Reaching to Heaven

Reaching to Heaven

A SPIRITUAL JOURNEY THROUGH LIFE AND DEATH

JAMES VAN PRAAGH

A DUTTON BOOK

The individual experiences recounted in this book are true. However, all the names and other descriptive details have been altered to protect the identities of the people involved.

DUTTON
Published by the Penguin Group
Penguin Putnam Inc., 375 Hudson Street, New York, New York 10014, U.S.A.
Penguin Books Ltd, 27 Wrights Lane, London W8 5TZ, England
Penguin Books Australia Ltd, Ringwood, Victoria, Australia
Penguin Books Canada Ltd, 10 Alcorn Avenue, Toronto, Ontario, Canada M4V 3B2
Penguin Books (N.Z.) Ltd, 182–190 Wairau Road, Auckland 10, New Zealand

Penguin Books Ltd, Registered Offices:
Harmondsworth, Middlesex, England

First published by Dutton, a member of Penguin Putnam Inc.

First Printing, February, 1999
10 9 8 7 6 5 4 3 2

REGISTERED TRADEMARK—MARCA REGISTRADA

CIP data is available.
ISBN 0-525-94481-8

Printed in the United States of America
Set in Palatino
Designed by Leonard Telesca

This book is printed on acid-free paper. ∞

To Regina, my mother

Whose eyes have shown me the beauty of heaven;
Whose words have taught me the language of the angels;
Whose songs have shared the music of the celestial choirs,
And whose love has brought me closer to the face of God.

Contents

❖

Acknowledgments

This book could have never materialized without the collaborative effort, inspiration, and hard work of the following kind souls, who dedicated so much of themselves to helping me pierce the darkness by illuminating these pages with heaven's golden light.

For the thousands from around the world, who wrote me with their words of encouragement and pain, this book is my return letter to each of you. I hope its pages will uplift your heart and bring you comfort and support with the knowledge that we *are* spirit, and spirit never dies. May all of your fears and disillusionment be transformed into courage and strength.

To the individuals whose stories are chronicled in this book, thank you for sharing your heartfelt moments. It is my desire that through your memorialized experiences of grief and suffering others will be touched by the same healing power of spirit.

And specifically to . . .

Linda Carwin Tomchin—who has truly given wings to my words and has supplied the ink to my pen, I thank heaven for sending me such a skilled angel.

Brian Preston—your love, support, and patience have enriched my life and taught me valuable lessons in sharing. Thank you for always taking the time to be there with a gentle smile, a helping hand, and a kind word.

Brian L. Weiss—whose friendship and support have been with me for lifetimes. Thanks for making it easier for me to

❖

reveal the truth despite those who use ignorance and fear to deny it. I look forward to discussing life's most profound quandaries over our next eight-thirty breakfast.

Michael J. Tamura—thank you for recapturing my missing parts with the numerous "tune-ups." You are a true inspiration.

Joseph Skeehan—your friendship, honesty, and trust are truly cherished. Thank you for believing in my mission and accompanying me on the long roller-coaster ride to the sky.

Ron Oyer—it's a big world out there. . . . Thank you for bringing its beauty and splendor to so many. The incredible places you have shared with us are just as sacred as you are.

Scott Schwimer—I will forever appreciate your magical eyes always looking out for me. I count on your honesty, loyalty, and friendship as prized treasures.

To Suzanne, Karen, Carol, Jennifer, Helen, Bob, and everyone else at ICM, thank you for your professionalism in getting every minute detail taken care of.

To Phyllis, Nicole, and everyone at PR with a Purpose— no one works as hard! Your dedication, friendship, and laughter bring joy into my life.

Thanks also to everyone at the Dutton for giving me the chance to open up the minds and hearts of so many. These rewards are far greater than can ever be measured on earth.

And for all my true friends, who stood by me wanting nothing more than friendship, thank you for not letting the glare of the lights spoil your perceptions, and for having the strength and courage to climb the next step.

Preface

I shall be telling this with a sigh
Somewhere ages and ages hence:
Two roads diverged in a wood, and I—
I took the one less traveled by,
And that has made all the difference.

—Robert Frost,
The Road Not Taken

I began my spiritual journey in the early eighties, and at the time I had no idea of what I would learn or how I could use my newfound perceptions in my day-to-day life. I had never planned to move to Los Angeles, nor did I plan to have a career as a medium. But when the door opened wide to the spiritual realms, and I walked through, I felt the Universe had called me to my destiny. I soon realized that my gift as a medium was to be used in the service of others. With the knowledge and understanding that at the time of death we will reap the rewards of our earthly thoughts and actions, I knew that lives could forever be altered. I was determined to bridge the gap between the physical and spiritual worlds by imparting the knowledge I had received about a greater spiritual existence. I felt that if individuals could learn from those on the other side and treat themselves and each other with dignity and respect while on earth, human hearts would awaken to goodness, and humankind would be relieved of so much suffering.

Of course, I am not the first to put forth such an effort. There have been many before me, and there will be many to follow. I honor every one of these pioneers. When one has the courage to forge ahead against the ingrained beliefs of a society, and to present ideas that actually threaten firmly established scientific, religious, and political paradigms, sometimes it requires great sacrifice. I have been blessed in my work because the potential to heal others and to reawaken minds to higher truths far outweighs any sacrifice on my part. I truly believe that as each one of us opens to his and her spiritual nature, our prejudiced and inconsiderate attitudes can turn into ones of love and mutual respect. Instead of opposing each other, we can celebrate our differences by knowing that we are spiritual beings sharing a common physical experience.

Spiritual enlightenment cannot be attained by waving a magic wand, or taking a class, or even reading a book. Nor can enlightenment be obtained according to a plan or a schedule. Each soul comes to his own truth in a personal, unique way and at the proper time. Our souls cannot be forced to grow, but like flowers, our spiritual selves can be fertilized and nurtured until they blossom and flourish.

Just as the dawn offers a palette of color, bringing a uniqueness and freshness to each new day, so, too, can each one of us bring a purity of heart to each day. Each new dawn is a moment of opportunity for us to aspire, discover, grow, learn, and serve. We are presented each day with a chance to expand our understanding of other beings, new ideas, diverse situations, and a variety of events. As we acknowledge and take part in these rich experiences, whether they are cheerful or burdensome, we can move through the cycles of life with a greater perspective on our foggy yesterdays, and certain anticipation of our tomorrows. Each dawn we can move one step closer to comprehending our own divinity.

I have written this book as a follow-up to my first book, *Talking to Heaven*. After its publication I made numerous appearances on television, and I was besieged with requests for information on the spiritual world. Since I no longer do individual sessions or counseling, I designed this book to be used as a tool for everyone—those already on a spiritual path and those who are new to spiritual ideas. For those already on a spiritual path, it will offer some helpful touchstones and reminders. For those venturing into an unknown world, I hope it can help hearts and minds open to the possibilities of eternal life, as proclaimed by those who have shared their profound insights and love from the other side.

Today is a new dawn and your next step on a journey inward to the eternal soul. Within the soul—right inside you—lies a whole new world of healing and hope, of familiarity and truth. To reach it you must journey along the road less traveled, but one that leads toward selfdom, independence, and empowerment—to the greatness that is you. With each step along the road, you will be on your way toward *reaching to Heaven*.

PART ONE

THE JOURNEY

I

❋

In the Beginning

But O the ship, the immortal ship!
O ship aboard the ship!
Ship of the body, ship of the soul, voyaging, voyaging,
    voyaging.

—Walt Whitman,
"Aboard at a Ship's Helm"

"**W**here do I come from?" How many times have you thought about your existence? Have you found a satisfactory explanation to your inquiry? Throughout the ages, philosophers, scientists, scholars, and religious teachers have tried to give satisfactory answers to the question of existence. For centuries pilgrims have traveled thousands of miles over treacherous snow-covered mountains for an audience with a sacred lama in hopes of learning the secrets of life. Others have searched for meaning in the galaxies or in the laboratory. Today, many of us seek such answers in churches, synagogues, and mosques, relying on our priests, ministers, and rabbis to supply such revelations.

And yet, I believe that within each of us lie the answers,

✿

in that invisible, undefined part called the soul. The soul is our spiritual core, the divine spark within us that was, is, and always will be. It has traveled the width and breadth of the universe, through all the eons of time, recording within it the lessons of a never-ending existence. It is the quintessence of who we are.

Unfortunately, all too few of us know how to tap into that light that burns so brightly inside us. Could it be that we've forgotten something so profound? Or have we been distracted, wandering in a labyrinth, validating our existence and measuring our self-worth by unhealthy family conditioning and distorted societal values? To reconnect to our true selves, we must escape this maze of external expectations. We must turn inward to listen to the voice of God—a voice that, once realized, gives meaning to life. We must recover our "sense of soul."

With that in mind, I have written this book as a sort of "portrait" of the soul as it journeys through life, death, and rebirth. In the first part of the book, I explain what it means to be spiritual, to be a soul living a physical existence, and how the mind creates its experiences. We will look at the various layers of the soul and how these parts contain a record of all its existences throughout time. The journey continues through the process of death. I will explain what happens when you die, where your soul goes, and the levels of existence that you may encounter in the spirit world, which vary with each individual. My purpose is to show that death is painless and natural and that there is nothing to be afraid of.

When we pass over, we are greeted by loved ones and spiritual guides who have been with us on many journeys. In the spirit world each soul chooses what it wants to experience. When we have achieved the fullness of our dreams and desires, and are motivated with joy and inspiration from the higher realms, we will make the decision to return to earth to live life once again. At birth we do not enter the physical world empty-handed; we bring along the wisdom of eternity contained within our soul's memory. Nor do we return alone; heavenly spirits are always nearby.

The messages from spirit in the second section of the book are designed to encourage you to examine the parts of yourself that keep you stuck in earthly illusions and unaware of your connection to the divinity within. As you will see, emotional blocks stunt spiritual growth and make our journey through life difficult. By reading about the trials and tribulations of others, you may discover the internal conflicts that hold you back from fully embracing life. Perhaps, the advice from those on the other side will help to alleviate your fears and urge you to heal your emotional scars.

In the last part of the book, I propose ways to help you take charge of your journey through life. There are meditations to achieve clarity of mind, and recommendations for fostering spiritual values in children so that they are well equipped to handle life's ups and downs. Finally, I offer the keys to unlocking the door to your spiritual self in order for you to remember who you are.

As we reconnect to our souls, our priorities about life may change. We will learn, as I have, that all the answers are within us just waiting to be revealed. As we open the door to the infinite, we will discover that we are all interconnected in this tapestry called life. Through the cycle of life, death, and rebirth, we learn who we are and why we are here.

❖

Opening the Door

Whenever I teach a class in psychic development or mediumship, I explain that it's much like taking a journey to a foreign city, such as Rome. In order to get the best out of the journey, we must prepare. To get to Rome, we buy a ticket, pack, go to the airport, find a seat on the plane, and get comfortable. If we don't know the language, we might want to bring along an Italian phrase book to help us communicate. We may also want to get a guidebook or join a guided tour so that we will be sure to see all the famous and historic sights.

In the same way, you must prepare for the journey to your soul. The first step is to close off the outside world of judgment and rationalization so that you can begin to tune in to the inner world of consciousness. This is not a new idea. For centuries, monasteries and nunneries have isolated individuals for this very reason. If individuals were kept away from society, they could not be contaminated by outside influences. Thus they could remain pure and receptive to a higher consciousness.

But how can we do the same when we are constantly being bombarded by outside stimuli? Every day we can't help but hear the latest news stories of violence, destruction, and illness, or gossip about movie stars and political leaders. We worry about the economy, how to save for our retirement. Our consciousness revolves solely around the happenings of a restless physical existence. We are so busy doing daily battle with the challenges that life presents us that we don't have the time to quiet our minds and acknowledge the fact that we are all spirits on personal paths to enlightenment.

To begin your journey, you must attune to an inner

world. The visualization that follows will help you do that. After you have read the next few paragraphs, put down the book and visualize the contents. The best way to do this is by closing your eyes, to close off outer distractions and to focus inwardly.

Meditation

As you close your eyes, I want you to become aware of your senses. Be cognizant of everything going on around you. You may hear the noise of traffic, or neighbors talking, or the sound of someone's television that is too loud. Try not to let such distractions bother you. You don't have to judge them. Just let them be what they are. Now, I want you to focus your mind by concentrating and bringing your awareness into your body. Feel your back against the chair, and become aware of your arms, legs, and torso as well. Concentrate on each part of your body. Notice how your feet feel on the floor or in your shoes. Be aware of how your clothes feel on your body. Is something too tight? Just observe it; don't try to fix it. Just let it be.

Now take a deep breath and slowly let it out. I want you to become aware of the breath. As you breathe in, realize that you are taking in oxygen. Oxygen is required for our physical bodies to sustain life on this planet. Oxygen molecules surround us all the time wherever we are. As you take them into your lungs, imagine the oxygen molecules invigorating every part of your body. As you exhale, see the old, stagnant air leaving your body. Its work is done and is no longer needed. The next time you take in oxygen, see it as energy. You may imagine this energy as stardust or snowflakes or any image that assists you in bringing the idea of this energy alive. As you see your image of energy, begin to focus on it. Eventually, experience this energy running inside and out of your body.

As you continue to visualize this energy, imagine that it permeates every form of life in regions throughout the world, perhaps from a mother holding her baby in Africa, or a priest saying his rosary in the Vatican. As you continue to imagine this energy, see it flow through a thoroughbred horse at the finish line of a race to a million ants building an underground colony beneath your house. The energy is shapeless and commonplace. It is bound by nothing and encompasses everything. It has no allegiance to a particular religion, nationality, belief system, intellect, or economic class. It is one with all. Think about that. You are a part of this energy and one with all no matter how different you think you are. You can't see the oxygen, the energy of life, yet it is here and there at the very same time.

As you continue to read, keep this newborn awareness of sharing one source within your consciousness. By doing this simple exercise you have begun to focus your mind on the concept of being one with all. This energy is a vital part of your life and your spiritual connection to everything and everyone.

2

❀

Awakening Your Mind

They are makers of themselves by virtue of the
thoughts which they choose and encourage; that mind
is the master-weaver, both of the inner garment of
character and the outer garment of circumstances,
and that, as they may have hitherto woven in ignorance
and pain, they may now weave in enlightenment and
happiness.

— James Allen,
As a Man Thinketh

E verything is energy. Science describes energy and
how it works in physical terms, based on earthly elements: how particular arrangements of atoms cluster
together. But it is on a higher level, in the fourth or spiritual
dimension, that we find the force that actually holds the
atoms together. This energy is what I call the God Force
energy.

Our entire universe is permeated by this God Force energy. It is what we are made of and where we come from.

The God Force energy is the center of all that is.

The mind, the spirit, and the physical body are all composed of the same God Force energy; however, each is vibrating at a different frequency. When I am asked if the mind is a part of our brain, I say the brain is the organ of the mind, just like the eyes are the organ of vision. Our sight is as good as the health of our eyes, and the same may be said for the mind and brain. The brain is organic, personal, and individual. The brain is constantly evolving; it is up to each of us to develop and increase the power of our brains. The mind is already perfect. As Emerson described the mind:

> Mind is an ethereal sea, which ebbs and flows; which surges and washes hither and thither, carrying its whole virtue into every creek and inlet which it bathes. To this sea every human house has a waterfront. But this force-creating nature, visiting whom it will, withdrawing from which it will, is no fee or property of any man or angel. It is as the light, public and entire to each, and on the same terms.

The mind seems to be the window to nature itself. The phenomenon of the mind can create, imagine, and reason. When we harness the positive energy of the mind, its results are nothing less than incredible. Take, for example, writing or painting. Writers and artists begin with an idea of a certain story or picture, and then transform it onto paper or the canvas. How did it get there? The brain can deliver only what is put into it, much like a computer. But the mind is a source that goes beyond our computer-like brain. It is linked with the God Force energy that encompasses all things. When we think of how Mozart composed an opera or a piano concerto, we think of him tuned in to some heavenly orchestra. As he listened to the music in his mind, he used his brain to write down the notes. The brain was the conduit through which he was able to compose, but it was his mind that created such musical splendor.

By understanding that the brain is not the source of ideas, and the mind is, we must also understand that each individual mind is connected to the Universal Mind and shares in its substance.

The Universal Mind

When I think of the concept of the Universal Mind, I find it easier to envision it as an enormous lake that is translucent, impressionable, and reflective. I think of the individual mind as a fish swimming in this lake. The fish is interdependent upon the environment it inhabits and is affected by its environment. Thoughts are like ripples upon the water. Each ripple originates within the lake and is part of the water, but each is distinct and individualistic as well. Each ripple affects each fish and thus the whole lake.

The Universal Mind has no boundaries or limitations, and anyone can use it. Have you ever watched a program on television and thought to yourself: I had that idea a year ago. So often people appear to come up with the same design or idea independently of each other. Why? Because the creative person tapped into the Universal Mind and pulled into her individual mind that particular inspiration. Ideas are merely sensations imprinted deep inside us. Once they are realized, we can take action. In other words, our brainstorms are vibrations from the Universal Mind.

When I first came to Los Angeles, my goal was to become a television and film writer. I remember waking up one morning with an incredible idea for a screenplay. It was

❖

one that I thought was unique and would have great appeal. I immediately went to my computer and began typing away. My story involved a children's book with characters that came to life and actually interacted with the author. I thought it was so unusual that I dared not tell anyone about it, even my friends. I didn't want someone stealing my idea. I completed the script in three months and sent it around to the various studios, and received the same reaction from each one. I was told that there were three other scripts with exactly the same story line. I was crushed. My unique idea, which I took pains to hide, had taken hold in the minds of three other complete strangers.

This unison of ideas among us is as genuine as the air we breathe and the sunshine we feel. On a global level, we all share in a feeling or a sense of one another. How did we all feel when Princess Diana was killed? There seemed to be a blanket of sadness covering the entire world. Even though most of us never knew her personally, on a soul level we could all share the pain and empathize with the loss because we are all connected. Just as the same sun shines on every individual, we all share a oneness and a commonality. We all share senses; we feel, see, hear, touch, laugh, and cry. We all share the God Force energy. Wouldn't the world be a better place if we were to think of each other as spiritual beings and shared our earthly paths with kindness and encouragement?

The Thoughts We Create

Thoughts are things! Thoughts are as real as the organs in your body. What sorts of thoughts fill your day? Are they friendly thoughts or hurtful thoughts? Thoughts are powerful, so it is important to pay attention to what you think about day in and day out. The life you are living is the result of your thinking.

Science credits certain patterns of neurons in our brains with forming particular ways of thinking and rationalizing. Yes, this is true. There is an element of electrical activity taking place within particular areas of the brain that affect our performance. However, the truth is: Thought is not created in the brain whatsoever. We don't say: Something comes to brain. Rather, we say: Something comes to mind. Thought is a function of the mind, and the end result is found in the brain.

There are basically three sources of thought. The first kind, while easy for some, is more difficult to come by for others. It is thought through prayer or silent meditation. The vibration of these energy thoughts is quite high. The first step in attuning your awareness to this higher frequency of energy is to make it a habit to set aside time for prayer and meditation every day. Although it may not always seem that anything is going on, in time you will find that the rewards of your spiritual practice are great. I believe becoming aware on this level creates a sense of humility, calmness, self-love, and joy.

During my years of training to be a medium, it was imperative for me to meditate daily. By aligning myself with this God Force consciousness, my connection to the spiritual dimensions heightened and increased in vibration. However, I had to sit patiently day after day in the silence to raise the level of my awareness of the God Force energy within me. Then when I read for my clients, I worked from a very high vibration of love. Mediumship itself is an incredible and miraculous ability, but the work takes on a

whole new purpose when the medium is developing on a
spiritual level as well.

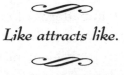

Like attracts like.

This is a concept I use often and to which I will refer several times in this book. When a person is centered and
thinks thoughts of love, peace, and abundance, he will get
back the experiences of those thoughts. Stop for a moment
and imagine everyone in the world thinking good thoughts.
It is sort of mind-boggling, isn't it?

As a medium on a spiritual path, it is most important
that I spend time in meditation and focus my thoughts on
the positive aspects of life. I believe that is why the messages that come through me are more spiritual in nature
and more accurate, and the lessons behind the communication are more beneficial to all concerned.

The second category of thought comes from our environment. We have to be aware of the great influence our
environment has on our daily lives. How many times have
you walked into a room and felt something not right? Or
how many times have you felt depressed or ill for no apparent reason? The reason is that you are picking up someone else's thought energy.

I always have had to be careful when visiting people in
hospitals because I am so sensitive to the sentiments and
feelings of others. Often, when I walk down the corridors
of a hospital, the cries of patients penetrate my mind: "I
want to get out of here," or "I don't want to die," or "I'm in
pain, won't somebody help me please?" The sense of sick-

ness and suffering permeates the atmosphere, and sometimes I become overwhelmed by it.

Like a radio station, we are continually sending out and receiving signals. We not only receive these signals from one to the other, but also, on a much larger scale, we are surrounded and influenced by the signals of mass consciousness. Although some of these thoughts may be quite good and humane, most are messages of greed, anger, selfishness, and dishonesty. These thoughts are attracted by and attached to the lower parts of our nature. With this constant bombardment of lower-consciousness influences, ideas of a higher, spiritual nature have little mass appeal.

This does not necessarily mean that all thoughts received from others are negative in nature. Healing prayer and love are higher thought vibrations and are also reflected in your surrounding atmosphere. When you send out love, a person receives that love. That love may not be detected on a conscious level, but it is nevertheless very alive and effective.

The final group consists of our most common, everyday thoughts. Psychiatrists and psychologists from Sigmund Freud on have broken down consciousness into three separate but interdependent levels of thought, the conscious, the subconscious, and the unconscious. The conscious mind is the one we use to count our change at the market and to read this book. The subconscious mind controls all the involuntary processes of the body, i.e., the regulation of sleep, respiration, digestion, circulation, etc. It never sleeps, and therefore never stops. The unconscious mind is unseen and vast. It is the warehouse of all past experiences, including everything we have ever thought, felt, learned, or witnessed from the past to the present.

However, it is the subconscious mind that runs our lives

most of the time. The subconscious is like a hardworking factory machine that is responsible for the regeneration of cells that heal the body. This part of the mind does not reason or rationalize—that job belongs to the conscious mind—but instead is tirelessly at work registering thoughts and impressions without judgment. As children our subconscious minds registered the words and ideas of the adults around us, and these memories are very much alive within us. Habits, among other things, arise from subconscious thoughts. In order to be in control of your life, you need to take charge of the way you think both consciously and subconsciously. There is great wisdom in the subconscious mind. If you begin to work with it, it can be of tremendous benefit to you and serve as an endless reservoir of knowledge.

Through our minds, myriad great discoveries and inventions can be achieved that can bring great benefit to the human race. When utilized positively, the human mind is a source of great works of art, philosophy, and science that truly improve the quality of life on the planet. But the mind that creates such amazing wonders also has the capacity to destroy and annihilate. It can impose terrible forms of cruelty and hatred. We owe it to ourselves to lift our thoughts to the highest frequency so that we can evolve to a higher consciousness and bring the splendors and miracles of life to future generations.

James Allen, a great teacher, who wrote a groundbreaking book called *As a Man Thinketh*, which I recommend to help you begin to change your thinking patterns. As Allen says:

> *Man is made or unmade by himself . . . in the armory of thought he forges the weapons by which he destroys himself;*

he also fashions the tools with which he builds for himself heavenly mansions of joy and strength and peace. By the right choice and true application of thought, man ascends to the Divine Perfection; by the abuse and wrong application of thought, he descends below the level of the beast. Between these two extremes are all the grades of character, and man is their maker and master.

3

❋

Getting to Know You

Yet the timeless in you is aware of life's timelessness,
And knows that yesterday is but today's memory and
  tomorrow is today's dream.
And that which sings and contemplates in you is still
  dwelling within the bounds of that first moment which
  scattered the stars into space.

—Kahlil Gibran,
The Prophet

What do we really know about ourselves? Our physical bodies, of course, are easily perceived, and we are very familiar with the domain of mind and thought that we explored in the last chapter. Beyond these realms lies an aspect of our being that is more mysterious, our spiritual nature. For this leg of our journey, it is important to keep the door open to all our senses, including our intuition or inner compass.

To begin, I want to introduce you to some of the language of the land of the spirit, the various "bodies of man" that make you a unique individual. These bodies are invisible layers of the soul's spectrum and are encompassed in the "aura." The aura can be thought of as a blueprint of our spiritual, emotional, mental, and physical energies and experiences. It is perhaps the closest externalization of the soul that one can observe.

The Aura

When I was a small child, perhaps six or seven, I remember telling my mother that I saw *lights* around people. My mother just smiled at me and went on her merry way. Because I didn't know what these lights were, I thought everyone could see them. They came in a variety of colors: blues, pinks, greens, yellows, reds, etc. I remember that I loved to shop with my mother in one particular grocery store because the man behind the counter always had such pretty colored lights around him. I would stand and watch the lovely rainbow of blues mixed with purples and pinks that surrounded him. I recall that he had a great big smile, and was constantly telling jokes to his customers. I guess this man with the lights stuck in my mind because he always handed me a lollipop before we left the store.

I had similar experiences when relatives or family friends came to our home for a visit. I would watch the color and lights around everyone, and say something like: "That man is green," or "That lady has a lot of brown lights around her." No one paid much attention to the comments of a little boy, other than to say, "You're so cute," or "Isn't that sweet." I also noticed that the lady with the brown lights didn't smile very much either. Later, my mother would confide in me and say, "The lady with the brown lights is very sick." Most of the people, however, were affectionate and loving; they were the ones who hugged and kissed me a lot. I would especially see bright pink lights around them.

❈

As I became older, my ability to see lights around people slowly vanished and occurred only occasionally. But there was one time particularly that I will never forget. I was about eight years old, and some friends and I decided to go to the local delicatessen to buy lunch. After we paid for our heroes, we hurried out of the store. I was the last to leave, and as I walked out the door, a tall man, not realizing I was there, knocked into me. I looked up, and he stared down at me; his eyes penetrated me like laser beams through a brick wall. Suddenly, I became aware of a misty black and gray cloud around the top of his head and in the front of his chest. Three days later, I saw the same man again, this time in the newspaper. The police had arrested him for robbing the delicatessen! That bit of news gave me a good scare. However, I still didn't understand what those lights meant until much later.

The aura is composed of layers of energy. When I was a young boy, I would pray for snow every night during the winter because it usually meant a day of play. Every morning when I awakened, I would run to the window to see if my prayers had been answered. When they were, I could hardly wait to go outside. But first my mother would begin the long and arduous process of bundling me in layers of clothing. First, I put on my T-shirt, then a long-sleeve shirt, then a bulky sweater, and finally my overcoat. The layers of clothing served a purpose in protecting me from the cold. So, too, the layers of the aura serve a purpose by recording all our experiences, feelings, thoughts, and desires.

This idea of the aura, or vital energy emanating from and surrounding the body, is not new. One of the very first Westerners to observe and write about it was a sixteenth-century alchemist and healer known as Paracelsus. He referred to our energy field as "a fiery globe." In the eighteenth century the Austrian physician Franz Anton Mesmer defined animal magnetism as electromagnetic energy that surrounded the human body. He believed this electromagnetic energy had an amazing effect on physical health, and that it could be transmitted from one person to another. In this century London physician, Dr. Walter J. Kilner, invented a machine made of dicyanin (a coal-tar dye) that was used to observe ultraviolet light. With his machine Kilner noticed a light around the human body. Eventually, he believed that one could diagnose a person's physical maladies by studying this light. In 1911 Dr. Kilner's research was published in a book entitled *The Human Aura*. In 1939 a Russian electrician, Senyon Davidovich Kirlian, introduced a photographic process by which unexposed film was used to photograph a particular object. When the film was developed, various kinds of "halos" appeared around the object. This procedure, known as Kirlian photography, is still used today, but it is mostly linked to psychic phenomenon, as scientists have not yet figured out how or why these "halos" or "auras" appear. There is one important thing to remember with this photographic process. Since the aura constantly changes depending upon a person's emotional, mental, physical, or spiritual state, a photograph can capture only the aura at the particular time it is taken.

My own ability to perceive auras remained dormant until I reached my early twenties. It was at that time in my life that I began to meditate and develop an inner awareness, as well as a rapport with the feelings and sensations of others. After years of discipline my ability to perceive auras grew tremendously. Today, this ability continues to play a large part in the work that I do.

When I do demonstrations, I usually see a vast array of

colors and lights. The color and intensity of the lights are different with each individual and vary with different parts of the body. If I notice a bright red light around someone's left shoulder and neck area, I know that this person suffers from headaches or neck problems. If I see an accumulation of a dark and dense gray or brown color near a person's stomach, I usually ask if there is trouble in this area, and usually the person will reply yes. Throughout my years of study and observation, I have learned that the aura is a very accurate projection, or mirror, of various conditions of a person's health.

But your aura reflects much more than your physical state. In fact, it consists of various levels of consciousness that make up your beingness. It is a representation of your innate character, an indication of your potential, as well as a record of your experiences. By the time you reach adulthood, your aura has gone through years of emotional, mental, spiritual, and physical experiences. Your abilities, desires, likes, dislikes, feelings of success, feelings of failure, as well as extraordinary happenings, upsetting or sad times, have all shaped your aura.

The size and shape of the aura depends on a variety of other factors as well. Usually, the aura is oval in shape, and extends beyond the physical body approximately twelve to eighteen inches. If someone is outgoing and expansive in nature, her aura will tend to be larger in size. For instance, when a person speaks to a large group, and tries to reach them, or bring them into her consciousness, the aura of the speaker expands to encompass her audience. That is what happens with politicians, preachers, musicians, actors, and orators who have to connect with their audiences. The opposite effect occurs if a person is introverted or shy. The aura does not expand; rather, it remains close to the physical body. Our aura also expands and grows when we are in an environment that pleases us. Moreover, I have seen a person's aura right before death, and it tends to be quite faint, like a line drawn around the body. This makes sense because at the time of physical death the aura withdraws.

Colors

When I see auras, I often see colors. One of the clearest and most common colors I see around people is green. Many times at demonstrations I have asked a person whose aura is filled with green, "Are you a medical worker or healer?" The reply is usually yes. Most people who work in the healing arts have bright green, healing auras. Remember, too, a healer is not only a doctor or nurse, but can be an individual like yourself who has an empathetic and receptive nature to anyone in need of help.

The colors of the aura vary with each individual. The brightness, hue, and tone of colors can range far beyond what we see in the physical world. The strength of the color is directly associated with the strength of the emotion behind it. Colors often vary on a daily basis. The following are some of the main characteristics of the aura's colors:

Red: Energy, life force, and strength. Physicality, anger, hyperactive, deep rage. Sexual.

Orange: Self-esteem, pride, and thoughtfulness. Ambition, self-control.

Yellow: Intellectual, mindful, optimistic, and happy. Indecisiveness.

Green: Compassion, healing, peaceful, prosperity, and sympathy.

Blue: Spiritual, devotion, loyalty, philosophical thoughts, and creativity.
Violet: Love, highly spiritual, intuition, and wisdom.
Indigo: Spiritual aspirant, benevolence, highly intuitive.
Pink: Unconditional love, friendship, and sincerity.
Gray: Depression, sadness, fear, and tiredness.
Brown: Greediness, self-involvement, opinionated. Grounded.
Black: Lacking vital energy, lower influences, ignorance.

Past Lives and Memories

While observing an aura, I also find that it tends to be composed of tiny geometric designs and patterns. These patterns can be interpreted as thought forms and are reflective of an individual's thoughts, either current or from the past. In other words, a person's past emotional scars will be reflected in the designs of his aura, along with desires not yet realized, or desires from the past. Through the years I have observed that these desires appear in the top right part of the aura. This area is linked to the mental part of an individual, and is where desires and goals are stored.

Furthermore, the aura embodies the accumulation of karma from previous incarnations, and the karmic lessons that we will endeavor to master during this current lifetime. All these things make up a person's true essence. In my first book I discussed the idea of karma in detail. For the purpose of clarification here, suffice it to say that karma is the concept of cause and effect.

On one of my spiritual odysseys, I saw clearly how past lives are reflected in the aura, and I got a karmic lesson of my own. Dr. Brian Weiss, author of *Many Lives, Many Masters,* and I once held a workshop for about three hundred people aboard a cruise to Mexico. Dr. Weiss is a distinguished psychiatrist who has assisted many people through his work in past-life regression. After finishing my demonstration one morning, I attended his workshop, though I had no intention of participating in the group. Not wanting to disturb anyone, I just sneaked into the back of the room and sat down to watch.

Dr. Weiss began his demonstration of hypnosis and past-life regression. Through various exercises people went back to certain past-life experiences. To my surprise, I, too, experienced several incredible past-life experiences. In one particular regression I saw myself as a general in several wars. I observed myself standing among my soldiers, and as the wars changed, so did our uniforms. From that regression I saw that I was responsible for ordering my soldiers to kill other soldiers. I was in charge; I had to make the ultimate decision that caused thousands of men to die in battle. As the scenes unraveled in my mind, I instinctively knew why I was here this lifetime: I had to alleviate the karma from those past lives when I ordered the mass destruction of all those men. As a healer in this life, I am balancing out past-life karma, repaying my karmic debt. In helping people to recapture their spirituality, I am here to right a wrong, so to speak, as well as regain my karmic balance, heal my soul, and move along my spiritual path.

After the exercise Dr. Weiss asked people to stand and share their experiences with the group. As individuals spoke about their past lives, I began to see a sort of tapestry of colors and patterns above their heads and to their sides. As I looked closer, I noticed that each square in their auras had movement within it. Each square represented a past life. If that wasn't enough, I also observed that a cord emanated from each square, and this cord attached itself to a certain part of the person's anatomy, e.g., to a leg, or heart, or head. Later, I asked several of the participants if they had physical trouble in the various areas in which I saw the cords attached. The majority of them said yes. The rest were unsure or could not remember. Some thought about it and remembered that they'd had a problem in that area earlier in their life. It was extremely clear to me that our past-life experiences, and perhaps even our future lives, are entirely present in the aura.

Environmental Influences

The aura may also reflect outside forces, positive and negative, that affect us. Practically everyone has had the experience of meeting someone and feeling either an immediate rapport or a terrible aversion. Why is this? In most cases we have tuned in to a person's energy field and received some kind of energy emanations. The result is that we are either in harmony or disharmony (and all the feelings in between) with these emanations.

Being in a church or place of worship usually fills us with feelings of peace and comfort. We seem to have a sense of harmony and oneness from the place. That's because we are probably registering the loving, spiritual feelings from the people who have worshiped there. Conversely, you can walk into a room or a house and instantly experience an unpleasant feeling for no apparent reason, only to find out that there was a fight or argument prior to your arrival. Again, something happened, and your aura "picked up" the energy that remained in the room.

❧

⮐

The mental atmosphere that surrounds us is impressed not only with the thoughts and feelings we create, but the thoughts and feelings of those around us.

⮐

This idea is very important. Every day we pass through a multitude of invisible yet powerful thoughts that have a definite effect on the physical state of our bodies. Thoughts always reflect the nature of the person who gave them life. Therefore, pay attention to the people with whom you most often associate. We are the company we keep.

Many times someone's personality is so overwhelming that, depending on our own emotional, mental, physical, or spiritual levels (especially if one or more are weak), the other person's energy will enter our electromagnetic space. Fortunately, we are all born with a sort of defense mechanism within the auric field to keep out other people's energy patterns and thoughts. In the final section of this book, I describe how you can protect yourself from someone else's wandering thoughts and emotions.

It is also very important to realize that the living do not monopolize our atmosphere. Discarnate beings, or spirits, also impress us and leave their thoughts within our aura. This is why so many times during the day, suddenly and for no reason, you start thinking of a loved one who has passed over. It is more than likely that the loved one is attempting to influence or impress her personality and thoughts into your electromagnetic field.

❖

The Bodies of Man

Within the aura are layers and compartments too complex to describe in detail here. The chief ones correspond to the four distinct "bodies," interpenetrating one another, that metaphysicians believe make up human beings.

These different layers are called: the etheric body, which deals directly with physical processes; the astral body, the home of feeling processes; the mental body, where all thought takes place, including psychic and intuitive thought; and the physical body.

The Etheric Body

The etheric body is also known as the *body double* because it duplicates, or takes the form of, our physical body. The etheric body is composed of a matrix of energy that interpenetrates the physical body at various points. These points, or energy vortices, are known as the chakras. The word *chakra* is Sanskrit for "circle." Through these chakras the God Force energy, or prana (also Sanskrit), enters the physical body to nourish various physical organs and the nervous system. You may want to think of the chakras as spinning wheels of life because they have a direct effect on glands and organs such as the pineal and pituitary glands, thyroid, parathyroid, thymus, adrenals, pancreas, liver, spleen, and the gonads. When our chakras are healthy with God Force energy, they appear in the etheric body as swirling circles of luminescent color. Therefore, the physical health of the individual can be observed in the etheric body via the chakras. The chakras are held together by lines of force that create a grid-like appearance, much like graph paper used by architects and draftsmen. Thus, these swirling circles of energy can be compared to a magnetic field, and one of the main currents of energy runs vertically up and down the spine and affects the nervous system directly.

Three years ago, a young man of thirty-eight came to me for a private reading. His name was Bob. After my customary introduction I picked up a pad and began to draw Bob's etheric body to determine his physical condition. At first I drew a stick figure. Subsequently, guided by my intuition, the pen moved slowly up and down the figure, but as I reached the lower half of his torso, the pen stopped. Bob's energy seemed to become all cloudy and dark at that point, as if it literally ceased to flow. I immediately told him, "You seem to have some sort of problem with the area around your large intestine." I stated that I felt his energy had been cut off. He paused for a moment, then looked at me and said, "Two years ago I had part of my colon removed. I have to wear a bag." Although Bob's health had improved, he still continued to worry and torment himself about that particular area of his body. I explained to Bob that his continued worry was causing an additional obstruction in his energy flow.

Persistent thought patterns and unexpressed emotions ultimately manifest in our physical bodies. In other words, what you think and how you feel materialize in some form, whether as health or disease, in the physical body. Think of your body as a train terminal and your thoughts as trains. These thoughts have to end up in the terminal sooner or later. That is why it is so important to keep your thoughts healthy, so your bodies stay healthy as well.

Bob's etheric body was acting as a barometer for his physical well-being. By tuning in to his etheric body, I was able to detect his physical condition. There are alternative-health practitioners who are able to identify ailments and illnesses exclusively through the perception of a person's etheric body. The etheric body especially corresponds to the frequencies of our physical body, while the other energy bodies correspond to other regions of our consciousness.

The Astral Body

The astral body is also known as the emotional body. This body is made of a three-dimensional ethereal material and is the densest body next to the physical. The astral body actually is an exact replica of the physical body, and extends outward from our physical bodies about five to eight inches.

Many metaphysicians, including Theosophists, use the term astral body interchangeably with the etheric body. Personally, I see the two as slightly different. As the etheric is concerned primarily with energy systems (the chakras), the astral is involved one step further with the emotional part of the individual. The astral body is made up of all the thoughts, emotions, and desires in your mind. All your earthly yearnings, significant memories, and core desires inhabit the astral body. At death this body leaves the physical and resides in the astral world.

So often I say to people in my seminars, "Why are you so afraid of death? You do it every night!" The truth is that when we sleep, the astral body leaves the physical body and travels into the astral world. It is the same with the concept of astral projection, except in this case the astral body leaves the physical body at will. So when I say, "We die each night," I mean we leave our physical bodies, much the way we will leave them at the time of our death. So, too, the astral body spontaneously leaves the physical body in situations involving accidents, or when under the influence of drugs, or when a person goes into a coma. When a person is unconscious, he is more than likely floating through the astral world.

Many times souls will work on the astral level while their physical bodies are at rest. I believe that when I do my work, a part of my astral body leaves my physical body and penetrates the astral world. That is how I can receive the strong emotions and desires of those loved ones who have passed on.

The Mental Body

As the astral body is concerned with the emotions of an individual, in a like manner the mental body is concerned with the thoughts of a person. The mental body is composed of an even finer etheric substance than the astral body, and extends from the hip line upward and outward.

The mental body is believed responsible for the transference of high mental energies that are too refined for the other bodies. These energies are of a sublime spiritual nature, and are transferred via the mental body in the form of psychic information, such as inspirations, gut feelings, and hunches. Many also believe that this body is made of two parts: a higher mind, which is shaped by thoughts emanating from the Universal Mind, spiritual concepts and higher truths, and abstractions; and a lower mind, which is concerned with material, day-to-day processes.

I believe that an individual who is recognized as a genius, or indeed someone who is highly intelligent, is a person whose mental body has evolved through lifetimes of experience and awareness. The soul recognizes this level of mastery and utilizes this awareness in lofty mental concepts and visions. Scientists, philosophers, and teachers are among those who apparently have the ability to contact the mental body in extraordinary ways to benefit the good of many.

Keep in mind that we exist concurrently in the emotional, mental, and spiritual bodies while we journey through life in our physical selves. These bodies intermingle and are dependent on one another, and make us whole beings. When we begin to understand the totality of ourselves, it becomes easier to understand that, in death, we merely shed our various bodies so that we can rise to higher planes, as we will see in the next few chapters.

4

✿

Death—the Way Home

I sent my soul through the Invisible,
Some letter of that After-life to spell:
And by and by my Soul returned to me,
And answered "I Myself am Heav'n and Hell:"
                                        —Omar Khayyám,
                                            The Rubáiyát

"What exactly happens at the time of death?"
That is the one question I have been asked
most often over my many years of work as a
medium. Unfortunately, I cannot give a definitive answer
because the experience of death is as individual as the experience of life. And although spirits have repeatedly tried
to answer this inquiry to the satisfaction of their question-
ers, the explanation of death is far beyond anyone's limited
scope of words and finite intelligence. How can we understand something that is outside our human awareness?
Even the best medium can only hope to describe with complete accuracy all the feelings a spirit wants to communicate about the process of death. Our human condition of
predisposed religious belief systems and societal attitudes

about death blocks any awareness that may come close to a true comprehension. Death has always been the greatest of mysteries. We can only imagine, read, pray, and theorize on what actually occurs, but we will never know what it truly is until we experience it ourselves.

As I write this chapter, years of séances come to mind, and I can recall specific details from hundreds of spirits that have passed over. It is the accumulation of these insights combined with information that I have obtained from a multitude of international books, papers, and materials on the subject that I share with you. It is as honest and objective an examination as I can give you about the experience of death.

Fear of Dying

Why are people so afraid of death? The answer is simple. It is an unknown experience. Most of us are too uncomfortable to talk about death, let alone think about the prospect that one day we will be dead. Up until now few people have taken the time to investigate the process. In recent years, however, there have been many individuals who have gone through what is termed a "near-death" experience and have reported their impressions of what it is like to die. So far there are quite a number of good books on this subject, particularly *Life After Life* by Dr. Raymond Moody. The details of near-death experiences in these books, such as *going through a tunnel*, or *meeting a loved one*, or *seeing a bright light*, or *encountering a spiritual being* are all very similar to the picture that is painted by the spirits that have come through my readings. The overall feeling shared in near-death encounters is one of peacefulness, the sense that death is not "the end." Death is just another natural process of life. We start dying the moment we are born and continue to die every day. On a physical level, cells degenerate, die, and are replaced, yet we think nothing of it. As I mentioned in chapter 3, we "die" every night when we go to sleep. This is the time our consciousness leaves the physical body and travels to the astral world. When we reenter our bodies the next morning, we return with memories of our journeys and encounters in the form of our dreams. We may not understand our dreams or what transpires when we sleep, but it doesn't matter. Life is happening in one form or another whether we comprehend it or not.

So what does happen when we die? The most significant insight that has been reported from those who have passed over is:

❧

At death we are aware that we
are more than just our physical bodies.

❧

Departed beings sense immediately that the physical part of them is a very minor component of that which they are, and that they are a part of all existence. By this time spirits completely understand their own intricate piece to the universal puzzle. They begin to relate to the whole picture and have no more need for dissension with or segregation from another fellow being. They see God in all things.

Many spirits have communicated through me that death itself was easy, but dying was not. Anyone with a terrible illness like cancer or AIDS may suffer intensely as the disease eats away at various organs of the physical vessel. Slowly, the prana, or breath of life, is drained from the body. This can be quite painful. But when death arrives, there is *no more* pain or discomfort. Pain is a *physical* condition, contained in the physical body. The memory of the condition might stay within a spirit's mental body, but purely as a memory; the feeling is gone. The condition will no longer have an effect on the health and well-being of the spirit body.

The Process

As we all know, there are different ways to die, or in more correct terminology, there are various ways to exit the physical body. But no matter how the transition is accomplished, one clearly goes through a physiological and chemical change. At the time of death, the spirit body is immediately encased in an etheric sheath, or its body double. The spirit remains in this state for a brief time before the etheric double is shed as well. This divestiture of the etheric body occurs at the time that the spirit actually leaves the physical body. Once the etheric body is shed, the astral body takes over. In its astral form the spirit is able to enter into the more refined energy of the astral world. No matter what the manner of death, this process always remains the same.

Spirits have often described how natural they felt at the time of death, and how in some cases they did not even realize that they had passed. I recall a reading I had with a mother and daughter. At the time the mother was dying of cancer. Her daughter wanted her mother to be reassured that when she passed, it wouldn't be painful. The reading was very successful. The mother heard from several spirits, including her second husband, who told her, "Don't worry. It will feel very natural when the time comes." The mother

❖

passed three weeks later in her sleep. Several months after that the daughter came for another reading. Her mother came through and was extremely grateful to her daughter and myself for helping her to realize what death would be like. She said, "It was just like everyone described—very easy and peaceful."

What I have stated is the general idea; however, I will now go through the process one step at a time.

Natural Death

Individuals who die of natural causes, or of an illness in which they are aware of the oncoming death, have typical transitions. Several days before the passing, their consciousness slowly begins to expand or amplify. They experience a kind of "keenness" of their senses, especially that of hearing and sight. Many have reported going through "a flashback," in which they see and feel every situation of their lives very clearly. During the flashback they are able to fully comprehend the reason for each life experience. It is at this point in a life review that the spiritual part of a person imposes some sort of self-judgment. By judgment I don't mean choosing between heaven and hell. Rather, spirits becomes profoundly aware of their actions and are quite sensitive to their treatment or mistreatment of others. They immediately recognize the "right" way they could have behaved. Hopefully, they will also see the good they have contributed to others as well. This life review happens in a matter of seconds and remains an intricate part of an individual's spiritual fabric.

Also around this time, dying individuals will often become aware of long-dead relatives or close friends who may be standing by their bedside. These spirit beings may be there to watch over or call to them. There have been many cases when a dying person will suddenly call out to a deceased family member or describe a scene. When Thomas Edison was in a coma and very close to death, he momentarily awakened, looked up, and stated: "It is very beautiful over there."

Right before the end, a dying person may experience a strong decrease or complete end to the pain in her body. The person may slowly fall into a coma, or may remain aware until the "final" moment. If she is aware, she may notice a sense of "coldness" in her extremities as circulation slows down and the God Force energy begins to withdraw from the body. As the withdrawal continues, the person may experience a feeling of "light shaking" or "tingling." This sensation is caused by the etheric threads that are beginning to loosen from the physical body in preparation for the body double's departure. At the moment of death, respiration ceases, and the soul leaves the body. At this point the "silver cord," the etheric fiber that nourishes the spirit while in the physical body, is severed. The spirit is free at last!

Suicide

In the case of suicide, a spirit *cannot* be harmed. Anyone who forces himself to leave the body prematurely will find that, although he can destroy his body, he cannot destroy his soul. The spirit self remains very much alive! Not only is such a being alive, but the "problems" that caused this act are still very much a part of its mental and emotional mindset.

Once a spirit understands what it has done, it is usually filled with a sense of remorse and becomes depressed. I believe that many of these tortured souls are mentally and/or emotionally ill. If a person has a mentally ill condition while on earth, she will need a great deal of compassion and understanding in the spirit world. So will an alcoholic or drug addict. The degree of need, love, and consideration varies with every situation. Often, there is work to be done with addicted souls because an addiction is carried into the afterlife. Suffice it to say, if such a soul is willing, spiritual teachers and healers are ready to assist in any way to bring it peace of mind and well-being.

Fortunately, the prayers and loving thoughts from family and friends on earth for such souls help to change the auric atmosphere of depression and torture into one of healing and love. That's why it is so important to pray for those who pass over. Eventually, these souls will become aware of their higher spiritual natures and will begin to seek a way out of their situations. There are many on the other side of life whose sole responsibility is to assist these trapped victims and lovingly escort them to areas where they can receive proper comfort for their mental torture. Above all, these spirits must learn how to forgive themselves.

Sudden or Unexpected Death

In a case of death by accident, violence, or natural disaster, etc., the spirit is forced out of the body so quickly that it barely realizes what has occurred. A spirit feels no physical pain from this kind of death. In all of my experiences, no spirit has ever reported that it felt pain going through a windshield in a car crash, or felt the crush of a tumbling wall during an earthquake. In this kind of death I believe a spirit is literally "knocked out" so quickly that there is no time to register any discomfort or pain. By the time a spirit comprehends its situation, it is already gone from the physical body.

Depending on the particular passing, a person might lose consciousness, or have a spontaneous awareness that he is standing outside of his body and is looking down at his lifeless form. He still feels very much alive and thinks he is a physical being until the realization sinks in that he is not. Spirits have often conveyed to me that they tried in vain to speak to the people around them and became disconcerted when no one answered back. Although we cannot hear the deceased, they are completely able to hear what we are saying and thinking.

Right after death it is customary that a departed family member, or spirit guide, comes to greet the deceased individual and assist her in her adjustment to the unfamiliar conditions of the spirit world. However, in the case of sudden or violent death, it may take awhile for the deceased to accept the situation.

Group Death

When groups of people die together in tragedies such as a bombing, a plane crash, or a natural disaster, they leave as a soul group. They are fulfilling what is termed *group karma*. In other words, on a spiritual level people decide to die together to burn off karmic debt. Remember that I am talking about the spiritual implications of such circumstances. As humans we all share in the pain of such a tragic loss of life. In chapter 7 I discuss how we make these types of spiritual decisions before we incarnate. For now, try to understand that these kinds of tragedies are all a part of our spiritual destiny on earth.

❀

When death is sudden and unexpected, individuals are usually unconscious and forced out of the physical body upon impact. There is *no pain* when such an event takes place. The spirit leaves before the physical body can feel anything. Please believe me when I say that in this type of situation no one feels hurt at the time of death.

Because this kind of death is a shock, and people are not prepared to make the transition, their spirits may stay at the scene and wander around to try to figure out what happened to them. Some may wake up in a kind of hospital setting. Others may think that they have escaped the disaster altogether and are still alive. In tragedies of this proportion, individual souls usually need assistance and comfort to make the spiritual readjustment to the afterlife.

Once these souls become aware of their circumstances and begin to question their situation, spirit guides or family members will appear and gather them together and lead them to a sort of reception arena. In this gathering place guides who specialize in this particular type of trauma will assist the newly arrived and troubled souls and explain the meaning of their situation. Some spirits will completely comprehend the facts of their death and make the transition easily while others will need further assistance. Spirit beings that work with psychological and problematic situations will help the latter to accept their new spiritual existence. Usually, problems are resolved when deceased family members or friends reunite with a newly arrived spirit. The memories of love help to free a spirit's mind of the tragic situation.

❖

Earthbound Entities

Once the spirit has shed its physical vehicle, it resides in its etheric counterpart. In this state the spirit has an immediate feeling of peace and freedom. Likewise, there is a strong sense of lightness and buoyancy because the weight and gravity of the physical body no longer exist. The spirit remains in this gray, misty etheric double for a very brief time, perhaps just moments, before the etheric sheath is shed and the spirit moves into its astral form. In a way you could say that the etheric sheath is a bridge from the physical to the astral. In most cases this transition is swift.

However, when a spirit is very close to its family and is not ready to accept the fact that it is dead, the earthly ties become a type of entrapment. In such a situation a spirit will stay very close to its corpse. Often, it will make futile attempts to communicate with family members. It is quite common for this type of spirit to attend its own funeral. Many times this act helps a spirit to realize it is no longer a part of a physical existence. By then it is finally ready to move onward to its spiritual home. Occasionally, however, a spirit gets "stuck" and becomes what is referred to as "earthbound." Often it is a person's belief system in life that keeps him "earthbound" after death. Let me explain what I mean by a person's belief system.

Once upon a time there was a man named Bill, who lived on the planet earth. He was an agnostic; he had no religious or spiritual beliefs. Bill was certain of only what he experienced. His attitude was, "When you die, you die. There is nothing more." During his life Bill was solely concerned with two things: himself and his possessions. His main purpose in life was to accumulate as much money

❀

and as many possessions as possible, even if it was through exploitation of or detriment to others.

One day Bill dies and awakens on the other side. He quickly realizes that he is not really "dead," just in another, lighter form. However, he still possesses his earthly, materialistic mind-set. With great impatience he tries to hold on to his possessions, only to find that he cannot. He does not understand that the etheric, gray, dull mist in which he is engulfed is a mere shadow of his former physical world. Unaware and unprepared, Bill continues to roam the earth as a ghost, visiting his house and contacting his family in an attempt to communicate with them. This "in-between" state may last a few hours, months, or even years, depending on Bill's desire to leave the physical behind and move into the astral or higher realms. Fortunately, none of us have to go through the same etheric entanglement as Bill if we maintain some sort of higher spiritual awareness.

A few years ago, my knowledge of earthbound entities came to me firsthand through a friend. Mike was a college professor who taught world history. He was so rational that he could not be convinced that the spirit world existed. Mike knew the type of work I did and even sat in some of my séances, but he didn't believe in any of it. Even when I conveyed messages from several of his deceased relatives, he didn't give them much credence. Looking back, I realize now that he sat in those séances merely to appease me. During the course of our friendship, Mike was diagnosed with a terminal disease and became quite despondent. I reassured him time after time that life doesn't end, but nothing I said helped him to rest easy. In time he became bitter and reclusive.

Mike died not long after his terminal diagnosis. Two days after his transition, he paid me a visit from the spirit side. I remember it vividly. It was early morning, and I was suddenly awakened by the appearance of a six-foot etheric body shimmering at the foot of my bed. I couldn't get over how real Mike looked, even down to his blond hair. He stared at me, then telepathically asked, "Am I dead?" I sent back my thought, "Yes, Mike, you are." He replied, "Thanks." On that note he disappeared. Immediately following his departure, I perceived the presence of an African woman dressed in incredible tribal robes. I knew instinctively that she was one of Mike's spiritual guides. I heard her say to me, "Thank you. He had to hear it from someone he knew." Then she, too, vanished into the ether.

The sad thing is that the world is filled with earthbound entities. Some, like Mike, realize right away that they are "stuck" and quickly move into the spirit world. Some aren't so fortunate. These earthbound entities roam the physical plane and "haunt" the living by influencing weak-minded humans. They are "caught" in between the world of the flesh and the world of spirit. It is unfortunate that our restrictive and rigid belief systems don't die when we leave the physical body. Instead, these convictions prove themselves true on the other side.

Earthbound conditions can also occur if a person passes out of the body violently. Here again, a spirit is lost because it is unprepared and doesn't realize what has occurred. In many situations like this, a spirit will often continue to do what it did on earth until it realizes that the body is dead, and it has passed to the other side. Spirits have often expressed anger at such untimely deaths; some even want revenge. Fortunately, there are spiritual beings whose job is to help these lost spirits cross over to the higher expression of life.

The transition from the physical world to the spirit

❃

world is natural and painless. However, our culture has built this event into one of immense fear, and people are not properly prepared for it. This causes spirits to become earthbound because they don't know where they are when they get there. That is why it is so important that we gain an understanding of the phenomenon of death—so that everyone's transition will be easy, gentle, and complete. We need only grasp that death is a doorway to life everlasting, and that there is *more to come.*

5

❀

The Spiritual Realms

Hence, in a season of calm weather
Though inland far we be,
Our Souls have sight of the immortal sea
Which brought us hither,
Can in moment travel thither,
And see the children sport upon the shore,
And hear the mighty waters rolling evermore.
—William Wordsworth,
Intimations of Immortality

As Wordsworth so beautifully expresses, we are on an endless journey between here and heaven. As with any journey on which we embark, there is always the anticipation of having an exciting adventure. Wouldn't it be nice to look upon our life's last journey as nothing short of the same? The truth is that we have taken the journey many times before and will take it many times again.

When an individual leaves the physical world, she leaves behind a heavy, dense body that has inhabited an equally dense, heavy world. Such a transition can be compared to removing a winter overcoat, or a snake sloughing off its outer skin. In essence, we do the same. When we die, we are finished using our human form, and so we let it go.

Nothing is lost except the physical body. The complete soul self remains intact; the astral, mental, and spiritual bodies are still alive and well. Even our personality, with all its feelings, likes, dislikes, emotions, and desires, stays the same.

Entering a New World

No matter how spiritually evolved a person has become, he begins a new existence in what is known as the astral world. In many ways the astral world is as solid and as real as the physical earth—a kind of etheric counterpart to the earth. This invisible (to our physical eyes) world interpenetrates and extends around the earth and is made of etheric energy that vibrates at frequencies beyond the physical spectrum. The astral world is composed of a number of levels, and each level corresponds to a particular etheric frequency.

The level of the astral world that is closest to the physical earth can be described as a type of reception area. This region is significant to newly arriving souls for two very important reasons. First, it provides an environment that duplicates the earth in every way possible. As a multidimensional existence it possesses houses, buildings, universities, concert halls, gardens, lakes, and everything that is recognizable to our material minds. This eases the shock of passing out of a solid, physical world. Second, it is a place that allows a spirit to become accustomed to the afterlife slowly. In the astral world, a spirit begins to live a more rarefied, spiritual existence and must eventually cast off its past earthly memory patterns, behaviors, and desires.

A newly arriving spirit will gravitate to the particular

❖

level of the astral world that corresponds to the frequency of its astral body's vibration. It will enter encased in a very real and tangible astral body, and will be as real there as it was here.

A Spirit's Point of View

I have had many opportunities to bring through messages regarding the conditions encountered by spirits when they entered the astral world. The following is a wonderful example of such a reading. It is a fairly typical story of a spirit's entry. But please keep in mind that there are different types of arrivals just as there are different types of deaths.

A young woman came to see me about contacting her mother. She was quite skeptical about the whole thing. She was feeling guilty that she had not been present at her mother's passing and wanted some sort of proof that her mother was all right. Her mother's name was Molly, and this is her description of her entrance into the spirit world:

"I remember it all felt very strange. I can only describe it to you as if I awakened from a dream. I found myself in a sort of hospital. Well, it seemed like a hospital, but it was very nice and cheerful. I knew or remembered that I had been in a hospital and couldn't breathe, but that hospital seemed so dreary and cold. This one was quite the opposite. I didn't feel sick anymore, nor did I need any more oxygen. I felt so well; I wondered where I was. I looked around the room and saw other people in beds, too. It all seemed so natural. That's the only way to describe it—natural.

"The man across from me said that he thought he was

dead because he knew that he had been in a fire. I heard him say, 'I bet we're in heaven.'

"Then a lady came into the room and walked up to me. Her eyes were so blue; I couldn't believe they were real, but they were. She spoke to me with what seemed to be so much compassion, but not in words. It was a sort of mental telepathy, yet I could hear and understand every word she was saying. I felt strange at first, but there was something about her that seemed very familiar. I couldn't place it. As soon as I had this thought, I heard her speak to me in my head.

" 'It's me, Jennie. We played together on the farm when we were little girls.'

"I couldn't believe it, but as I looked into her eyes and saw her sweet smile, I knew she was right. It was Jennie Gallagher. We played together as children. I remembered that she died from rheumatic fever when she was eight.

" 'How can you be here? I thought you were dead!'

"She mentally told me, 'I am dead. You're dead, too!' For a moment I was shocked. Then Jennie reminded me how close we had been as children and that I was very upset and angry when she died. I even asked God to take me to heaven with Jennie.

" 'When we were children, we made a pact, remember? Whoever gets to heaven first would come to welcome the other one! Well, here I am!'

"As she told me this, the memory flooded my mind as though I had just thought of it, and suddenly I was filled with a supreme sense of joy and happiness. At that point Jennie invited me to follow her.

" 'Where are we going?'

" 'Outside to the reception area.'

"I didn't understand why. 'But I'm sick!'

❀

"She laughed. 'That condition was all in your head. You are a spirit now and perfectly fine.'

"Before I knew it, I was out of the bed and sort of gliding toward the front of this hospital type of building. I remembered thinking how beautifully I was dressed, and Jennie told me that she had dressed me with her thoughts.

" 'Everything here is done with thought,' she explained.

"I followed Jennie out the doorway into a beautiful courtyard. It was filled with nicely dressed people; I felt as though I was in some sort of Easter parade.

"Jennie informed me, 'There are others waiting to see you. I'll see you later.'

"I walked down the stairs into the courtyard. It's hard to describe how beautiful everything was. It was more than a gorgeous spring day; it was perfect. Everyone was smiling, and I could actually feel the joy everyone was feeling. Children were playing in gardens that were surrounded by the most exquisite water fountains.

"The next thing I saw was a young couple standing at the bottom of the stairs. They were smiling at me. Here again, I thought I knew them, but they didn't look the way I remembered. They were young and perfect and as real as could be. I walked down the steps, and the closer I got, the more I recognized who they were. It was really them—my mother and father, Gertrude and Jed!

" 'I can't believe it's you,' I cried with happiness.

"My mother patted my head. 'It's all right, don't cry. You'll see how real everything is as soon as you stop thinking with your earthly mind and adapt to your spiritual self.'

" 'Why are you so young?'

"She told me, 'Once you pass into spirit, you can take on the appearance and age you feel most comfortable with. We picked our thirties because we enjoyed that particular time in our life.'

"We talked some more in the garden. I was feeling so good. Then I began to see other members of my family. There was my brother, Barney, my grandparents, my aunt, and my favorite, Uncle Jim. Uncle Jim had taught me how to ride horses on the farm. Everyone seemed so full of life. They told me over and over again to rest and enjoy a life free from health problems and the concerns I'd had on earth.

"I remembered telling them, 'It all seems so real, so very real.'

"Before long my mother took me to her house so that I could rest. It was the same house I had lived in when I was a little girl, even down to the kitchen curtains blowing out the front window. She took me to my room, which had a four-poster bed. It was the exact same one my father had built for me. I laid my head down on the pillow and began to fall into the deepest and most peaceful sleep I had ever known. Right before I sank into sleep, I remembered thinking, *Now* I know what the expression *Welcome Home* really means."

After two unbelievable hours, I finished the reading. I paused for a moment to thank my spirit guides, then looked over at Molly's daughter. She was calmly sitting with tears streaming down her face.

She muttered, "That's her, that's my mom. She did have a childhood friend named Jennie. She told me about her. And those were her parents' names. And she adored her Uncle Jim. She told me stories about how he used to teach her to ride horses. I know it is real now! I had a dream last week, and I saw Mom in that four-poster bed. In fact, I have a picture of her standing next to that bed. My grandpa built

❖

that bed for her. I am happy she is all right and is home." The young woman wiped her tears and put her arms around me in a hug of gratitude.

The Astral World

The world Molly's mother described is sometimes referred to as *The Summerland*. This astral world is in many ways as solid as the physical earth, although its energy is light and ethereal. When an individual soul makes the transition to the astral level of existence, it enters with its astral body. Like the etheric body that is shed at the time of death, the astral body is an exact copy of the physical body, complete with arms, legs, fingers, toes, etc. However, it does not contain any illness or infirmity. For instance, anyone who is blind or deaf, or in a wheelchair, or has a terrible disease that leaves the body in a deteriorated condition, will not bring these disabilities into the spiritual realms. No matter if an arm or leg is lost in an explosion, or a body is totally annihilated by disaster or war, a spirit arrives in perfect form. These afflictions are purely the effects of a physical body in a physical world. They are *not* the conditions of the spirit world or the spirit body.

*The spirit body is whole and perfect
and can never be destroyed or harmed!*

Although our spirit bodies arrive in perfect condition, our personalities, composed of accumulated memories, prejudices, yearnings, and sensibilities, do not change. In fact, our entire mental and emotional outlook remains completely unaltered. Everything that we have ever experienced in the physical world is inscribed in our soul pattern. It is ironic, in a way. On earth we spend so much time making sure our bodies look good and spend so little time on things that matter, such as improving our relationships or being true to ourselves. After we die, all the effort we put into taking care of our bodies won't matter because they will look great anyway. However, we will still be stuck with all the same problems and uncertainties that we thought would vanish with death.

A newly arrived soul finds itself on a spiritual level that is made up of the accumulation of character traits and various earthly experiences that it had created before death. In other words, a soul gravitates to a state of existence that contains its interests. Souls with matching interests join together on a similar spiritual level.

Earthly Illusions

One of the first illuminations that touches spirits upon entering the astral world is an absence of time.

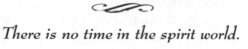

There is no time in the spirit world.

However, since a spirit has so recently passed from a world of clocks and calendars, the memory of time has a strong hold in its thought processes, and its natural inclination is to wonder what day it is. A spirit might think it has been out of the physical body for just a few moments when in actual earth time it has been gone for three days.

❖

Realizing this discrepancy confirms to a spirit that it is no longer bound by the limitations of the physical world. In the spirit regions time is not measured by the position of the sun and stars but by involvement in experience. A spirit literally has all the time it needs; it is more concerned with what it wants to do rather than the time it takes to do it.

Equally confusing to arriving spirits is the fact that in the astral world physical laws and boundaries, such as gravity and sound and speed, no longer apply. Spirits find out very quickly that they are not limited by a fixed world. In the fourth dimension and beyond, spirits are able to be in several places at the same time, and the mode of transportation is thought. Spirits have no need to speak because they can read each other's thoughts. As I have said before, all situations are created by our thoughts even in the life beyond.

Family members on earth assume that their deceased loved ones on the other side are privy to the entire plan of creation, and they expect all of heaven's secrets to be revealed. Often I am asked, "Why can't a spirit tell me the answers?" Or, "If she loves me, she would certainly help me out." The truth is that spirits love us enough not to give us the answers. They know that for a loved one to grow and advance, he must go through experiences without any sort of psychic hints. Spirits will not hinder our spiritual growth by telling us answers that rob us of the need to understand certain situations. We must live through our experiences in order to gain wisdom and fly higher.

While a newly arrived spirit does possess a keener awareness or an expansion of consciousness, its knowledge is limited to the spiritual level at which it finds itself. And as its consciousness expands, the most significant insight a spirit will gain is a broader realization of the harmonic oneness to everything. A spirit realizes that it is united by a common denominator to every other expression of life. The ingredient that makes all things possible is the unyielding and never-ending element of *love*.

A Time to Reflect

Along with this perception of unity, a spirit becomes cognizant of its entire soul composition. It knows clearly the complete history of all of its lifetimes of experiences. There is a point when a spirit will begin to judge and examine every experience, moment, and instance of its recently departed life. It probes every thought, feeling, and action taken, and views what has been a contribution to its soul's growth and what has been an impairment. In other words, it does a comparison report. It measures how well it has fulfilled the original soul plan.

In this reevaluation process a soul might realize that in order to gain the most wisdom from a certain experience, it might need to repeat a similar situation in a future existence on earth. This initiates what is referred to as the karmic process, i.e., a carryover of an experience from one life to another in order to gain spiritual awareness. This process is not meant as a punishment for doing something "wrong." It is merely a spiritual evaluation of the experience. If a soul believes it can redo the experience in a better way, it will return to do it over. A spiritual being recognizes its immortality; it knows that it is responsible for all conditions it has caused in the past and all those it will create in the future.

❖

The World You Create

There is a view that heaven is filled with winged angels playing harps and floating on clouds. This is purely a myth. A spirit's home in the spirit realms is a precise reflection of its life achievements and/or transgressions while on earth. After it has adapted to its new world, it is quite common for a newly arrived soul to be greeted by a spirit teacher and taken on a tour, so to speak, to witness the various levels and expressions of spiritual life. This excursion demonstrates how far a spirit has risen in soul consciousness as well as how it can attain a higher level of spiritual growth. There are as many levels of spiritual regions as there are mind-sets. So many times I tell people in my lectures, "You are responsible for creating your heaven or your hell based on your thoughts, words, and deeds." The environment is within each person. Ordinary people who attempt to live a decent life on earth by respecting one another and demonstrating love whenever they can have no need to worry about their afterlife existence. They will gravitate to a wonderful level of unlimited peace, joy, and love. Based on the multitude of readings I have done, let's look at what the average good-hearted person's environment might look like after she passes into spirit.

As you begin to look around, the first thing you would observe is incredible beauty. You would discover radiant, manicured gardens as far as the eye can see with each flower bursting forth in brilliant color. The vivid colors in the spirit world are beyond our natural, earthly spectrum. Everything in this environment is literally "lit up" and crystal clear. The light of the realm does not originate from any sun or star; it is known as the *Astral Light*. This illumination causes the colors to change in order to complement a particular type of environment. Because all things are harmoniously connected, you might think of this glowing effervescence as a reflection of the light that shines within each spirit.

The next thing you would notice is the scent. The rarefied atmosphere together with the sweet, flowered perfume of each bloom creates an angelic aroma. So often the spirits have said that they instantly possessed a heightened sensitivity to the exquisitely sweet smell of their environment. The unyielding scent and beauty of this heavenly expanse is beyond words to describe. It is a perfect world filled with rolling emerald meadows and magnificent forests. These bountiful trees need no pruning or care; there are no falling leaves. Everything is so alive and in harmony with every other part. This bit of heaven is a place where nothing is out of order, where everything is in accord.

Besides the beauty, there exist schools of knowledge housed in extraordinary buildings created with materials unfamiliar to our earthly minds. In fact, the buildings appear to have a translucent, opalescent quality. Perhaps that is where the term *pearly gates* derived.

Every type of education and instruction can be found in these great buildings—art, music, languages, philosophy, the sciences, or theatrical arts. Each hall of learning has its own *thought atmosphere*. This thought ambience is created from the feelings of the people enjoying their interests, and the love of the architect who used his expertise to design the building. Everyone shares in the intent of the building and the vision of the one who created it.

❧

Creating Your Home

You will even have a chance to create your own home setting on the astral level. Perhaps you would like to have a
small cottage with your own garden surrounded by a bab-
bling brook somewhere in the countryside. That is possible.
You will be able to conceive of and create your home with
your thoughts, or you can have an architect help you with
the design of it. Usually, spirits will build exact replicas of
their earthly dwellings because they feel more comfortable
in a familiar environment. But if a spirit chooses to be in a
palatial estate, it must have the consciousness to create it. If
a spirit had low self-esteem and a "poor me" mind-set on
earth, it is highly unlikely that it will create a palace in
heaven. Or if a spirit doesn't feel that it wants a big house,
even though it had one on earth, it can create something
completely suited to its taste, such as a cabin in the woods.
Whatever is constructed is *all* a reflection and representation of the particular soul's nature.

Living Your Desires

When we enter the astral world, our deepest emotions and
desires and our strongest likes and dislikes come with us.
These qualities are still very much a part of our being, since
we have not quite fully experienced them. So in spirit we finally get the opportunities to manifest and live out all our
dreams and fascinations.

For instance, let's say you have always wanted to paint
but didn't know how. In the astral world you can at last experience the joy and satisfaction that painting has held for
you. Perhaps you have always wanted to design clothes or
be a great chef. Here it is possible to fulfill those wishes.
Everything is created with thought, and all a spirit needs to

do is to learn how to breathe life into its thought, and a dream is realized.

In spirit you will be able to enjoy desires that have strong emotional and sentimental ties. The more fixed a desire, the longer you will keep it, or the longer it will take to release it. Once when I was doing a television interview, I did a reading for a young lady in the audience. During the reading her father came through, and she asked what he was doing. Her father told her that he was having a great time at the races betting on horses!

The host of the show glanced over at me with an odd look and said, "Oh, come on, you mean to tell me there is horse racing in heaven?"

I told him, "Well, for this man that is heaven to him. He enjoys it." The host cocked his head and raised his eyebrow as if to say *this guy is crazy.*

But the girl turned to me and gleefully declared, "That's my dad! He went to the track every Saturday!"

So you see, the astral world is arranged out of what we want, and what we feel we need. These desires are contained in the lower part of our personalities; they are not a part of the lofty spiritual side of our being. Once a spirit realizes that it does not need such a desire anymore, letting go of it is easy. The astral world is like a clearinghouse; it helps to wean us from our earthly emotional longings.

Letting Go of Old Habits

Not only do we keep our dreams and desires alive, we pass into the world of spirit holding on to our old habits as well. Since this particular spirit world is near the earth's atmosphere, our mental and emotional bodies still contain all the trappings of earthly life. Certain spirits continue to feel

✿

a need for their habits and addictions. For instance, it's not uncommon for a person who was a heavy smoker in his earth life to continue to smoke on the other side. Besides cigarettes, spirits will materialize alcohol, drugs, or their favorite foods. Many of the habits are so strong that a soul will experience them over and over until they are all *lived out*. Eventually, when a soul realizes that the habit weighs down its spiritual growth, it will shrug off the heavier coils of desire and lift higher.

The time spent in the many levels of the astral world varies with each spirit. Surrounded by the creations of its own desires and cravings, a spirit will remain in this region as long as it has an affinity to these energies. As a spirit cleans away the debris during its astral readjustment, it is, in essence, preparing for fresh opportunities when it returns to earth at a later time.

The Dark Land

Although it would be impossible to describe in detail all the levels that exist in the astral world, suffice it to say, there are some less exalted ones. In order to give you an overall view, I think it would be beneficial to describe one extreme condition of the astral level that has been called hell. This lower astral region is not a place of beauty and sweetness. Rather, it is a condition brought into existence by the thoughts, words, and actions of those who have produced pain and suffering on earth. All of us will reap what we have sowed. No one is exempt. So a spirit that has lived an earthly life of injustice, cruelty, and hate might find itself here.

This lower region vibrates at a much slower rate than

the upper regions. Here the light is dim and fades almost to a faint darkness. The atmosphere in this region resembles a scene right out of a Dickens novel. A pungent and unpleasant odor pervades it. Shadowy figures squirm from place to place in what seems to be an endless dance of restlessness. There is no safe refuge for a tormented soul when it is trying to flee from its own baseness. The astral body of a spirit in the lower regions is not the same as in the heavenly spheres. Sometimes it is misshapen or missing parts and appears to be destroyed and miserable. The dwellings on this level are not made of marble and stone but stacks of rotting wood.

Spirits in such a dark realm harbor mental attitudes of hate, malice, and the need for control over others; they are ruled by the lowest elements of the physical world. The inhabitants can be murderers, rapists, thieves, swindlers, cheaters, assassins, or anyone who has harmed another human being. We often think of these types of people as lost souls, and in a way they are, for they wander aimlessly and prey on one another. A soul remains in this darkened hole until all of its lowest desires are lived out. Only when it comes into spiritual awareness can it move to the upper portions of the astral plane. When such a depraved soul has the slightest inkling of wrongdoing, a spirit guide immediately appears to help it. No one is ever really lost because the God Force energy is within each soul.

There are many other caliginous places where spirits reside. They may not be as physically repellent as the one I have just described; nevertheless they are bleak. Like hell, these dwellings are molded out of negative mental attitudes and the darkness of spiritual ignorance.

❖

Like Attracts Like

The individual mind resembles a magnet attracting others like itself, and this universal law of affinity remains your compass in the afterlife. The beliefs and attitudes you hold dear are very much a part of your life in the astral world.

Here on earth you are literally thrown together with people of varied ideals, belief systems, and economic, racial, and ethnic backgrounds. Once you cross over from this earthly existence, you will be attracted to a state of being where everyone thinks, behaves, and lives the same as you. Therefore, you will find yourself on the same level with other spirits with similar belief systems. For instance, scientists, mathematicians, theorists, and philosophers might be on a comparable mental level with each other, for this is their reality. If a person has extremely strong religious convictions, she indeed will be in a place with similar thinking minds that perceive existence in the same way. Like minds will always gravitate together. Perhaps, this is heaven for most.

More important, this universal law of affinity unites us with loved ones that have passed over before us. We have been with these same souls many times before and will be with them many times hence. As we make our transition, they will be waiting to take our hand and show us the endless possibilities of life in the world of spirit.

For some individuals life in the astral world is brief, while for others, depending on their entanglement in physical urges, it is much longer. When a spirit is ready to ascend higher, it dies another death of sorts and travels to a new spiritual home, which some call "heaven."

6

❀

The Evolving Spirit

I hear beyond the range of sound.
I see beyond the range of sight,
New earths and skies and seas around,
And in my noon the sun doth pale his light.
　　　　　　　　—Henry David Thoreau,
　　　　　　　　Inspiration

I am often asked, "How long do we stay on the other side?" And, "Do we stay in one place, or go to other dimensions?" During my readings I can tell a spirit has evolved into the higher heavenly worlds by the way it transmits its thoughts and feelings. Many times I will say to a client, "I feel as though this man has been on the other side at least ten years," or, "This woman has just recently arrived." I can tell the difference by the clarity, or lack of clarity, of the thoughts a spirit sends and the type of emotion behind the messages.

For instance, a newly arrived spirit may transmit feelings and thoughts in a very urgent, highly charged emotional manner. Its personality traits are strikingly obvious as it conveys an "earthy" way of thinking. When a spirit

❖

has been in the spirit world for a longer duration, it will communicate quite differently. Usually, the transmission will be very calm; thoughts will be lucid and easy to understand. It will also convey messages that are balanced and meaningful for a loved one.

The astral world is like an intermediary step in a spirit's progression, a place where all the basic and lower emotional needs are lived out in their totality. As a spirit continues its journey, sooner or later it will become disenchanted with earthly dreams and longings and will begin to awaken to a higher aspect of its consciousness. When a soul is ready to lift higher, there will be a complete sloughing off of the old earthly memories and patterns of thinking.

The Higher Life

This releasing of the earthly patterns and lower elements of the emotional body refines and lightens a personality. As these old remnants are left behind to disintegrate in the lower astral regions, a spirit goes through another death of a sort. Hinduism and spiritualism actually call this a *second death*, when the lower bodies of an individual's spirit are cast off. This death enables a soul to advance to a higher spiritual sphere and become a more enlightened being. A spirit moves into the true Heaven world.

This "Heaven" is not a different "place," for there are no physical borders in the spiritual world. The "geography" is not delineated as it is on earth. Instead, there are different vibratory rates, and more evolved spirits gravitate to higher etheric frequencies. The higher the frequency, the brighter and purer the light of the land. When I say "land," I am actually referring to a *state of consciousness*. When spirits reach

❊

this higher frequency, they resonate with and reflect the glory of the divine harmonic essence.

In the higher realms everyone is at the same level of spiritual understanding, like a symphony of beings in tune with each other. For some this may mean a reunion with members of their earth family. For others it could be a meeting with former friends and lovers from previous incarnations. Still other spirits will be present that have never touched the earth but are familiar to the rest. Each member of the group contributes in its own way to uplift and better the others so all feel complete and whole when they are together. The term commonly used for such a spiritual family is *group souls,* or *soul group.* Such a group maintains a kinship through karmic ties and past earth life experiences. Spirit guides form a bond with this assembly and play an instrumental part in each spirit's life.

In this heavenly atmosphere there is no need to express thoughts and feelings because spirits of the higher light have total cognition. While on earth our thoughts and feelings can be hidden, this is *not* so in spirit. Every thought a spirit has is made visible and appears as its own unique light radiating from within. At this level of consciousness, spirits are much more than their recent personalities. They are complete and integral spiritual beings that have incorporated all of their earthly experiences and personalities into oneness with God.

Everything in the higher heaven realms is refined to the finest of elements. The light of all spirits blends into the divine light, and everything is one with this light. That is why it is difficult at times to get explicit details from spirits that have been in the higher realms for a long period of time. They are no longer attuned to an earthly consciousness.

Many evolved souls have come through the veil to

express to their loved ones the "lightness" and "fullness" of the world in which they reside by describing how everything in their environment is in unison and complementary to everything else. They have spoken of the perfect expression of a thought, or the epitome of a musical note, each encompassing the immense fullness of God's light.

It is a magnificent world filled with immense beauty and glorious landscapes. Spirits *feel* and share the life of every blade of grass, every leaf of every tree, and every petal of every flower. There is utter unison in this divine song. Music is not only heard but also completely experienced in every part of every being. The environments are radiant and are linked in a pleasing order and sense of oneness.

Even the buildings are created only with the purest materials derived from the highest qualities of mind. The structures are not solid but ethereal and shimmer in God light. It's difficult to describe their appearance; the closest images conceivably are holograms. A spirit may choose to have a house or place of residence at this level, but not for the same reasons as on the lower level, where they are created out of need or adornment. Everything is done for the sheer joy of it, and is a blending of the purest creative thoughts that express love of the divine.

A spirit may also wish to have a "physical" appearance in the higher sphere. It might decide to change its looks from the last incarnation to the one it lived hundreds of years ago, but any form it chooses will be perfect. It may choose to wear clothes but not like the clothes we wear on earth. The attire is rather dazzling and brilliant—the color and glow of the spiritual garments reflect a spirit's inner awareness. Clearly, the raiment is secondary to the intensity of light that emanates from within.

❖

A Healing Atmosphere

When a spirit first enters the lower astral world, it has an opportunity to live out its lower emotional desires. In the higher regions it has an opportunity to utilize the finer qualities of its mental body. A spirit will spend most of its time involved in the understanding and utilization of thoughts and ideas, which is an important step in its growth. By doing so, it actually supports the mental expansion of others on the lower and earthly realms. I have had the privilege of listening to spirits tell of their experiences in the higher regions. The following reading came through me during a trance state during a visit to a healing center in Brazil.

"The first thing that caught my eye were all the buildings. They reminded me of being in a big city, but not like cities on earth. Somehow this city was enhanced by its surroundings rather than depleted by them. Many of the buildings were alike in shape and style and complemented one another. They all fit together perfectly, as if they were snapped into place like pieces of a puzzle. The buildings seemed to be made of jewel-like substances, like mother of pearl and diamond. All the colors shone and blended in perfect harmony. The more I stared at these buildings, the more I realized that the light reflected the type of tasks being done in each individual structure.

"As soon as I wondered what was going on in one of the buildings, I found myself standing inside. The light was overwhelming. There was a huge group of souls sitting in a sort of arena-style theater. Each one was concentrating its thought toward the center of the arena, where another spirit was sleeping. I realized that this was a healing center. There was no need to speak because we could read each other's minds so easily. As I looked closer, I saw a beautiful

❖

violet and white light surrounding the sleeping soul. The spirits were sending this unhealthy individual divine light to quicken its vibration and lighten the dark areas that were caused by illness-producing thoughts. I realized that the spirit was someone from earth who was being healed during sleep. The spirits were helping this individual to return to a realization of the divine within. That's when it came to me that no one is ever lost in spirit, even those who are unaware of their light, like those beings on the lower realms of darkness and mental ignorance. I knew that the soul in the center would wake up with a new, healthy awareness of itself. You see, nothing was given to it; the soul was merely in the process of being awakened.

"Then I wondered if animals inhabited the spirit world, and my thought transported me to a hillside. There I watched as wild animals like lions and tigers dwelt side by side with their prey. It reminded me of that Christmas card—the lion lying down with the lamb. The most ferocious of beasts was as tame and as gentle as the most docile of animals. As I stood in awe of this miracle of nature, I heard the thoughts of the animals. I could understand their thoughts just like I could anyone else. They said that violence in nature did not exist in this place of pure harmony. Survival was no longer a part of their consciousness. I was surprised by the absence of domestic animals like cats and dogs. Immediately, I received the response that they were in places where they could run freely, or they were with their loved ones from earth. At that very moment I felt a complete rapport with every living creature."

❧

A Child's Life

The higher realms also contain nursery-like centers, where evolved spirit beings nurture and care for babies and young children who have recently left the earth. The caretakers and babies are drawn together by each one's capacity to love and be loved.

There are so many reasons why a young life is cut short and returns to spirit. Each spirit has its own divine destiny and a soul plan to carry out. Perhaps for a certain inexperienced soul, life was too difficult to fulfill, and it left the body rapidly. Many spirits have told me that this is what is commonly known as Sudden Infant Death Syndrome (SIDS). Perhaps, too, the karmic ties between child and family had to be accomplished through an abrupt end to life. For whatever reason, a soul will have a chance to learn and return to earth once again. Many newly born souls may decide to complete their "physical" cycle of life in spirit so that they can further develop high-minded qualities and principles. These babies will progress in the spirit world so that when they return to earth, they will have a new and expanded awareness of life. Others may possess such a strong desire to experience opportunities in the physical world that they will return to earth right away without properly maturing in ways to assist in the next incarnation. Again, whatever a child decides is wholly dependent on its soul development.

Infinite Learning

Souls in the higher regions are there to learn, to expand and develop their mental capacities and to receive instruction through their spirit guides and teachers. There is an infinite number of learning institutions depending upon which aspect of their mentality spirits wish to cultivate. However, the goal is not to get a Ph.D. in history or math. Spirits are schooled in truth. Truth is simple, yet it takes a great mind to understand its simplicity. Virtues such as love, humility, and patience are explored.

At the same time, there are many great intellects drawn together to work in the philosophical, medical, and scientific arenas. These minds unite to test the mysteries of the universe. They may contemplate how thought affects the physical world and the physical health of a being. Some may spend their time inspiring earthly inhabitants with perceptiveness and inventiveness. When spirits work with like minds on earth, they seed visionary thoughts that will be harvested in great new inventions and precious cures. Often, these humans are already tuned in to a particular spiritual mind-set. Any and all is possible if individuals are willing to nurture their own light and open themselves to the infinite possibilities of God.

The higher regions of light are truly mystifying. One learning center at these heights is particularly significant. It is in many ways one of the most important states of being and is crucial to our existence today. One evening during my development circle, I went into a full trance, and my astral body left my physical body and traveled to a place that I would like to share with you. At first I noticed an incredible marble-like building. All the walls were made of the same material, yet colored in hues that I had never seen before. Then I was seated in the balcony of what seemed like a huge theater or courtroom. All around me were people focused on the situation that was taking place on the floor below. As I looked down, I noticed men and women outfitted in various periods of dress. I recognized one figure sitting at a light table conversing with others. He looked just like

Benjamin Franklin. I thought it strange to be there, and wondered where I was. As I asked the question, the answer came to me just as quickly. I was in a hall of great minds. That is all I remember from the experience. When I came out of the trance, I asked the other members of the meditation circle what had occurred. They stared at me with dumbfounded expressions.

"Don't you remember?" someone asked.

"No," I responded.

"A man came through by the name of Franklin."

The class members then described how this man told them about the various injustices in the world brought about by man's self-obsession.

"He said that he was one of many in spirit who work with governments of the countries of earth to bring understanding and a common ground."

I thought the information was incredible and explained my vision in the great assembly hall.

Since that time I have read about similar visions described by other spiritualists. Let me share one with you. This particular vision is of a great temple, similar to those on earth in Greece or Egypt. This temple is reflective of the type of energy at work behind its walls. Inside you will find those who are of a high compassionate calling. Some are political leaders, others are notable inventors, while others are great humanitarians from the past. Still others present have never lived on earth; these beings are from different dimensions of our universe. All of these spirits are in the process of working with the minds of earth's political leaders, imparting ideals of peace, compassion, unity, and understanding. By fusing their thoughts together, they can help to enlighten men and women so that all hearts may awaken to peace and accord. Sometimes they succeed, and the world we know triumphs in policies of peace and justice. Other times their attempts fail. Trying to pierce minds of ignorance, darkness, greed, and deception with the greater truths of light, love, and justice is indeed a great challenge.

Although many powerful leaders succeed not by virtue of an open heart but by greed and dishonesty, spiritual beings do not give up on them. Evolved souls accept that all are created from the same element of light and love, and they continue to work on behalf of the whole human race. Even though we often wonder if our prayers are heard, they are. And they are answered. It is up to us to keep the door open to our hearts for guidance to enter.

Artistic Achievement

One cannot complete a tour of these realms without viewing another very important component of the landscape. This is the domain of artistic inspiration. In the marvelously intricate and gleaming halls of artistic expression, many masters are at work. It is here where these mediums of God's divine light synthesize and transform creative energy into materialized expressions of colors and words. Only the paintings of the highest quality are actualized. These paintings are truly frozen inspirational moments of color. One not only can view these works of art, but also completely *feels all the love* that flows from them.

There are also beings involved in the materialization of God's light through words. The most exalted thoughts are whittled down to a portion of their greatness to inspire creative writers on the lower and earthly levels. Words are merely manipulated energy pulled from various frequencies of expression. These expressions are materialized on an emotional level and conveyed as forms of encouragement, guidance, humor, and sadness. These plays, stories, poems, and writings are meant to spread light into the lower astral areas and earth to awaken each being to the divine. This is true of all expressions of creativity.

The last stop on our journey is to a place where the divine symphony is at work. The colors of the atmosphere constantly change from moment to moment in a veritable rainbow of radiance lighting up the heavens. However, these colors are not atmospheric like our earth sky, but emanate directly from the minds of the composers and musicians of this sphere. Here is heard the language of the angels in all its divine glory. Walking through these great edifices of light, we will see individuals scattered throughout, receiving healing vitality from the heavenly notes and melodies. Many musicians are fusing their thoughts and energies to create new expressions of sound for the well-being of others. These expressions are purely God's eternal, loving, and joyful light. So you can see that much lies ahead for a spirit on its journey home to God.

We will be forever developing the richness of our soul natures to manifest the love of God. Ultimately, for many of us, after we have completely filled our hearts with the light of Heaven and are so full with the oneness of spiritual love, we may decide to reenter the conditions of the dense, physical world. With the knowledge from these spiritual realms, we return to earth with a desire to inspire others with the insights we have gathered in spirit.

7

❀

Returning to Earth

> How like an angel came I down!
>   How bright are all things here!
> When first among his works I did appear,
>   Oh, how their glory did me crown!
> The world resembled his eternity,
>   In which my soul did walk;
> And ev'rything that I did see
>   Did with me talk.
>
> —Thomas Traherne,
> "Wonder"

As a spirit develops in the heaven realms, it aligns with the great Light of understanding. This beaming, celestial luminosity shines brightly from the center of its being, and is the trademark of its soul. Possessed of so much God consciousness, a spirit becomes attuned to the harmonic rhythms and divine laws of the universe. Yet within the soul makeup of every spirit there is a yearning to reach even higher levels of spiritual consciousness. This optimum growth is developed through myriad "soul lessons" and is exercised only by a spirit's free will. These soul lessons are mastered from opportunities experienced in the schoolroom called earth.

Two-thirds of the world's population believe in reincarnation or rebirth, the rebirth of the life force or soul in a new physical body. Although not accepted dogma in orthodox Judeo-Christian religions, early Christians, notably the Gnostics, also accepted the concept of reincarnation. By the time Christianity was embraced by Emperor Constantine in the fourth century, any reference to reincarnation or transmigration was removed from Christian dogma. In Hinduism and Buddhism, a soul returns to earth to work out lifetimes of karma. When it is perfected, a soul ceases the cycle of rebirth and returns to the God soul.

I am sure that most of us have had déjà vu experiences of being in a familiar place or with a person with whom we felt an instant kinship. I remember a time when I was driving through New Orleans with some friends and we stopped to have some dinner. I began to walk away from the group as if in a trance.

One of my friends asked, "Where are you going?"

I replied, "I want to see something. I have a very strange feeling that around the corner and at the end of the block there is going to be a white church with two steeples."

My friend just nodded and followed me around the corner. Sure enough, at the end of the block there was a white church with two steeples. The moment I saw it, I had an inexplicable sense of recognition. I had been in that church sometime before, but not in my present life. There was a *knowingness* about it that I could not explain.

In order for a spirit to receive the most ideal soul-growth experience and utilize its God-created energy, it must prepare for its return trip to earth. Therefore, a spirit will spend the duration between lives familiarizing itself with knowledge about the material level of existence. Because we are made from the God Force energy, in essence we co-create with God. It is up to us what we want to do with this energy. It is also imperative that we remember that effects are caused not only by physical actions but by mental actions—our thoughts and words. It is *all energy*! We decide how we want to use it! When a spirit feels ready, and *only* then, to re-experience a physical life, there is a natural progression of steps for its entry to earth.

The Etheric Council

To help a soul get ready for its next passage, there is a group of highly evolved beings in spirit that make up what is known as the Etheric Council. These beings have completed earthly incarnations and make recommendations to help other spirits develop their "life plan," the spiritual objectives a soul wants to accomplish in the upcoming life. This plan outlines the incarnation as a sort of blueprint of opportunities needed for a soul's advancement. The exact details of the plan are left to a spirit to decide. That is where free will comes in.

Each soul is unique. The knowledge and wisdom of each life is incorporated into its memory, so it might choose a vocation in an upcoming life that is familiar. For instance, I know that I have spent many lives perfecting the sensitivity, aptitude, and discernment for my spiritual communication. When I was regressed, I witnessed myself in life after life at religious and mystical endeavors. I saw myself as a Catholic monk, a Russian Orthodox priest, a Tibetan lama, a Buddhist monk, a gypsy, a metaphysical scholar, and a medieval seer. So it is not unusual that I am a medium in this life. It is the same for most of us. What we are doing in this life is probably something we have done before in some form or another.

❧

When we are born, everything that we need to fulfill our soul's plan is impressed into our etheric body. In other words, all the answers to all our problems lie within. Any trial or tribulation is merely a test to see if we can uncover the spiritual solution. A soul is given many opportunities to develop and expand by living through adversity. Growth is never easy and can be accomplished only by experiencing every aspect of a situation and fully comprehending it.

When a spirit looks at the physical circumstances of its next life, it realizes that some of them won't be easy but necessary for its growth. A spirit can see how such adversity can help its overall progress, or how such experiences will make another facet of its diamond light center shine. This is why living on earth is compared to being in a schoolroom. We are here to learn; once we are finished, we return home.

A soul decides how fast or how slowly it wants to advance. Certain spirits will stay on the other side until they feel absolutely ready to return to earth and face a difficult task on their journey. Others might be quite enthusiastic to jump into such a spiritual assignment because they know it will hasten their spiritual growth. Still others might think they could accomplish more at a particular period in earth time. The Etheric Council helps plan all aspects of a spirit's upcoming life and makes sure decisions are not made out of emotional desire but from spiritual need.

During the decision-making process a spirit may consult with other spirits that have been a part of its past earthly experiences, or that have karmic ties to it. These karmic ties may be positive or negative depending on what a soul wants to experience. As I described in chapter 6, there are soul families of like-minded individuals. In the case of a soul group, spirits may decide to come back and live out

❀

karmic obligations with each other. In addition, there are always groups of souls that return to earth during a certain period in history to fulfill karmic ties on a global level. These souls return to bring forth certain knowledge from the past. Depending upon their degree of spiritual consciousness, these spirits can either create advancement or deterioration for the world's population.

Karma

We are all familiar with the saying: "What goes around, comes around." This is another way of stating the universal law known as karma. The word *karma* is Sanskrit in origin and literally means "action." Within this law of action is built a natural cycle of cause and effect. Simply put, we have gone through lifetimes either sowing seeds or throwing rocks, and we will reap the effects of what we have created, good or bad.

Since there is no time in the multidimensional universe, the cycle of cause and effect may extend through lifetimes. The length of time spent on earth is merely an illusion because it is a limitation of the physical body and the physical world.

In truth, one lifetime is a very small period of time in the grand scheme of existence.

So the result of our actions today may not necessarily be settled in the same life or even one lifetime. It depends on the intent, power, and severity of the actions. All actions imbedded in the soul membrane will remain there until they are burned out and proper balance and equilibrium have been restored.

Many people have the point of view that karma is negative. This is not true. Think of karma as paying off a debt or balancing an action. Karma is really an opportunity for a soul to progress. Once a soul learns that its actions have consequences, it will no longer have a need to create difficult karma in the future. So by the time a soul returns to earth, it will have a life plan, karmic lessons encased in its soul memory, a chosen body, parents and family members, relationships, time and place of birth, station in life, and time and means of death, to say the least. These all reflect the kind of spiritual work it wants to accomplish.

The Rebirth Process

Although I have had extensive communication about a spirit's vacating the physical body, I've heard very little about the actual process of entering a new home. Spirits often tell me that they are preparing to come back to earth, but fall short when asked to describe the means. It could well be that spirits are not fully aware of the complex process, or that the phases and events that take place upon entering the physical world are impossible to convey in any language. I have had some spiritual insight about the rebirth process, and have read many books about this phenomenon, which I describe for you here. My information is based primarily on clairvoyant experiences, and theosophical and Eastern schools of thought.

The word *incarnation* means descent into the flesh. When a spirit has a desire to come back into the physical world, it will reactivate a specific part of its being known in theosophical circles as the *physical permanent atom* or the *physical seed-atom*. This seed-atom is a concentrated field of energy that is located in the heart chakra center. In this concentrated energy field is a full and complete karmic picture of the soul's earthly experiences. At the time a person is about to go through a karmic experience, this karmic picture is released as energy that flows along the meridians of the body.

This seed-atom is connected to what is known as the *life cord*, which is the last strand of the silver cord. This life cord is responsible for supplying the seed-atom with all the karmic information regarding a particular being. Where does the information come from? The karmic information is found in what is known as the *soul mind* or *monad*, which is the ethereal energy of total oneness. Are you still with me? The monad is a microcosmic expression of the perfect universe that each person innately possesses. It is our perfect God-like expression. I call it the "spark of God," or the God Force energy.

Once this seed-atom is activated through the law of affinity (like attracts like), a soul begins to create a sort of force field of mental and astral material around itself. This mental and astral material forms the mental body, and in so doing begins to limit the thought processes so as to fit into our earth mind. The mental body is patterned on what is seen and understood in the monad of the individual. It is important to remember that all levels of existence are connected and intertwined with one another, and several developments occur simultaneously depending upon the particular level of consciousness.

It is believed that the seed-atom units with a zygote or embryo at the time of conception, and the birthing process begins. The zygote and the seed-atom together emit a sound vibration that attracts energy on the etheric level. At the same time a spirit, which is still in the astral world, begins to embed its own vibrations upon the streams of matter entering the etheric, mental, and physical forms. It does so through a shaft of white light that flows between the heart of the fetus and the seed-atom of its new mental and astral bodies. At the moment of fertilization, this shaft of light descends from the soul heights into the sperm, irradiating it with energies that will set in motion the birthing process.*

By this time a soul has descended to the lower spheres of the astral level and begins to attract the etheric substance in order to build its etheric body. The etheric energy vortices or chakras begin to form in this gestation period as cells grow one at a time. During this period various spiritual beings and forces help create, formulate, and protect this infant being. In Hinduism these spiritual hierarchies are called *devic* or elemental beings, and in Christianity they are the angelic kingdoms. The soul remains in the astral world while its physical vessel is being formed. When the etheric counterpart is fully formed, a spirit will begin to lower its vibration of consciousness and descend into the region known as the *river of forgetfulness*. The Greeks refer to this as the link between the visible and invisible worlds. Immersed in these ethers, a spirit forgets its connection to divinity and all of its previous existences.

People often ask me, "Why is it that we forget who we are and where we come from?" My response is that it is done through God's grace. First of all, by not knowing, we are less homesick for our heavenly existence. Second, if we knew all our past mistakes and failures, we might obsess

Through Death to Rebirth by James S. Perkins

❖

over them to the point that we would not be able to progress and get our present work done. By forgetting the spirit realms, we start with a clean slate, so to speak. However, this karmic information remains a part of the seed-atom and can be unlocked as a person becomes more self-aware. Nothing is lost, just forgotten. Each of us has many opportunities to remember our true self. During the months that follow fertilization, various stages of physical development take place. Tissues, nerve fibers, and muscles are activated. It is during this period, when the muscles begin to move, also known as *quickening*, that a mother begins to take on a psychological sensitivity to the new life inside her. In the psychic realms, the devic and elemental beings continue their work in building and finalizing the physical form. It is at this quickening stage that a spirit recognizes its new vehicle because it feels a sense of pulling from the newly forming body. Besides this pull, the monad or soul mind that contains all karmic information projects itself into the embryonic atmosphere. A spirit will feel that particular current of energy and immediately come into an awareness of itself as part of this new being. Several months before birth a spirit will float around its new vessel, going in and out of it, as a way of trying it on for size. This is how a spirit becomes familiar with its new surroundings. It also has the opportunity to acknowledge any physical problems or defects with which it might have to live. Toward the final two months of pregnancy, a spirit's magnetic tie to its new body becomes much stronger, and it will spend more time in its new home.

The time of birth is very significant for a new soul. A combination of forces melds in complete synchronicity. The planetary, psychic, physical, and spiritual energies interact in total rhythm with one another. That is why the time and place of birth are of utmost importance, since such an astro-logical arrangement will help to determine race, family, and status on earth. There is a time and place for every-thing. Just like waves beating upon a shore, birth, like death, occurs in its perfect and natural time, even those we label "premature." At the precise moment, a spirit fits itself fully into its new body, travels down the birth canal, and emerges into a new world. It is ready for a life full of infi-nite spiritual opportunities.

Abortion

Sometimes in my readings a spirit will speak about the con-ditions of a mother's body and the importance of keeping healthy not only on a physical level but on the emotional, psychic, mental, and spiritual levels as well. An incoming spirit is linked psychically with its mother and picks up everything that is around and within the mother's aura. Once life is set in motion, nature takes charge and fulfills what it knows to do. If a mother does not want the child, these feelings are recorded in the aura and are felt by the in-fant. In addition, a psychological shock could easily affect the forming fetus in many ways, such as birth defects. In the case of miscarriages, I believe this is nature's way of ending an imperfection or defect of some kind. This may not be just of the physical body, but of an etheric or mental nature.

This brings me to the controversial and painful subject of abortion. Every time I speak, people come up to me to express their sadness over it, the sense of loss and torment-ing guilt. In a healthy pregnancy the forces are set in mo-tion and will continue to build a vessel until birth or termination. When an abortion takes place, a spirit has not fully invested the body and returns to the God world. It will wait there for another appropriate opportunity to reveal itself. Remember that a new being is spiritually linked to its mother and is completely aware that an abortion may occur.

In most of my readings concerning this topic, it seems that abortions occur for the mother's spiritual growth. Before incarnating, a spirit will set up a situation like having an abortion to work through lessons of self-worth, guilt, failure, and love of self. Is there a karmic effect on a woman in a future incarnation because of this act? Not necessarily. Hopefully, a woman will learn and grow in self-love and come to self-enlightenment because of such an emotionally difficult experience.

Living in the Physical World

As the remembrances of a heavenly world of joy and light slowly fade away and are replaced by a sense of heaviness and coldness, a newly arrived soul feels somewhat confused as it enters the physical world once again. It has been separated from a world of order and belonging; in its place is insecurity and loneliness. No longer is a spirit floating through a world of color, light, feelings, and wonderment. No longer does it travel at the speed of thought. No longer does anyone read its mind. A spirit is once more captive in a world where the energy is dense, the colors dim and drab, and the only light it sees emanates from a sun.

Although quite "old" when it reincarnates, in a way a spirit is brand-new. Yes, it carts along a package of karmic lessons, but it also has newly formed mental, emotional,

❖

and physical bodies with which to experience them. It will rely partially on its lower instincts in order to fulfill its physical needs. But what about the emotional and mental parts of this being? How will they be developed and fostered? Equipped with its spiritual life plan, a spirit must engage the world of flesh to fulfill its destiny. It must learn how to love, be hurt, and grow. The rest of its life on earth will be shaped by its relationships, religion, and the society in which it lives. Life has come full circle, and a spirit's journey moves forward through time once again.

PART TWO

SPIRIT
SPEAKS

A s a soul travels the road to perfection on this physical plane, it encounters peaks and valleys of circumstances that test its strength. Trials of self-mastery over the physical world are not always easy. Many times we would rather falter than go through the pain. But if we could only keep in mind that what awaits us at the end of our journeys is worth all the agonizing and arduous steps that we have to take, we would forge ahead gladly. We must realize that we are never alone; there are always loved ones and enlightened guides ready to direct us with support and strength.

Though there are myriad tests a soul must go through on this earth, the lessons of the heart are probably the most challenging. They touch the core of our being with the

❧

tenderness of love and the bitterness of pain. We expose our innermost parts to others and hope they will accept and love us. If they don't, we close down just a little bit, and each time we are rejected, just a little more. Then we begin to manipulate others in an attempt to be recognized and be treated the way we desire. It is our fear that holds us back from passing these emotional tests of self. We remain stuck in the illusions of reality until we take control of and master the emotional part of our being.

I have been host to many on this side of the veil who come to me carrying heavy hearts. They are seeking an opportunity to contact their loved ones one more time and place their unsettled emotions at rest. Many realize that they must handle these unresolved feelings in order to advance their physical, mental, emotional, and spiritual growth. This is true for those on the other side of the veil as well.

At this stage of the journey I would like to share with you several sessions that I feel represent some of the most common emotional trials and tribulations we have to experience. My hope is that by examining them, you will open your mind and heart to healing similar emotional situations in your life. Perhaps you can benefit from reading about others' mistakes and misfortunes, and avoid the need to experience the same pitfalls. At the very least, I hope you discover a new way of understanding yourself and others.

In respect to privacy, I have altered the names of the individuals involved but have remained true to the insights and messages revealed.

8

❈

Expectations

Everybody is unique. Compare not yourself with
anybody else lest you spoil God's curriculum.
                                              —Baal Shem Tov

If you are not true to the inner voice or the divine source
within your heart, you cannot be happy. How often
have we all said something or done something not entirely truthful just to be liked or to feel a kinship with another person, and then lived to regret it? This is only a
minor example of "people pleasing," but how many more
serious ones have we committed because we fear rejection?
Many people sacrifice their individual dreams to fulfill
someone else's desires for them.

I almost did. My mother's dream was for one of her children to be a nun or priest. I decided to fulfill that wish and
be the priest my mother always wanted. Why? Because I
thought this would make my mother proud of me and love
me all the more. However, after a year in a seminary I

dropped out, realizing that I lacked the spiritual calling in my soul to enter the priesthood. It was my mother's desire, not mine. I didn't realize then that my mother's love was always present and always would be.

When we are children, it's natural for us to strive for our parents' love, and for our parents to want to mold us into what they expect us to be. But for those who come from demanding or undemonstrative families, the effort to please may never end. As children grow older, the parents' wishes remain in their subconscious and become a part of their programming. As adults, self-worth may depend on trying to please others, as they once tried to please their parents to get their love. In the end, such adults never really live for themselves.

One of the most tragic—and all too common—situations I encounter in my work is a spirit coming through with remorse for an unsatisfying life. Fortunately, upon entering the higher life, spirits who find themselves in this predicament quickly respond to the unconditional love offered by the loving spirit beings that are present. These spirits begin to turn their regrets into insights, and they learn to see themselves as worthy. They appreciate the many tasks they accomplished and all the love they gave to others when on earth. How much better it would be if they could have expressed their true natures in life before it was too late. We have all been placed on this earth to discover our own path, and we will never be happy if we live someone else's idea of life.

It's a shame that so many of us have expectations about how things should or should not be, or how we should or should not be. The following are some examples of unrealistic or unrealized expectations. I find that many of these cases are very sad because in most of them the potential of the individual is never fulfilled, and there is great regret for a life not fully lived.

A Father's Dream

Two girls named Adrienne and Paula came to see me. I can only describe them as young, attractive California women, with long blond tresses that flowed down their backs. Looking at them, you would have never suspected that anything could possibly be going wrong for them. Yet there was something deeply troubling hidden behind their bright blue eyes. After sitting with them for a half hour, I had to say:

"I suddenly feel an incredible chill around me. It is giving me goose bumps. Do either of you feel it?"

They both shook their heads no, so I continued:

"I have an awful sense of sadness. It feels as if someone is crying."

The girls' expressions suddenly changed.

"I have a man here who seems to be very distraught. I don't know why. He keeps showing me a car. It looks like an Impala. I am not good at types of cars, but that is what comes to mind."

One girl slowly said, "Yes." The other began to sob.

"This man is telling me about the garage, about being in the garage."

Now both girls cried softly.

"Do you know someone by the name of Carl?"

"Yes, that's our dad's name. Is he all right? Please tell us."

The feeling of sadness worsened. "It is me, he says. He is saying Carl with the car."

"Yes, he collected old cars. They found him in his black Impala. Oh, God. Is it him?"

❖

"Yes, it is your father. He is with someone named Frank. He was happy to see Frank. Frank has been there for a very long time. Your father is telling me that he missed this Frank. God, he is someone who has been over there many, many years."

The girls shook their heads, and the one on my right spoke:

"Frank was his brother, who died when they were children. That was over fifty years ago."

"I am sorry, but I must tell you, your father is a very sad person. I get the feeling that he worked too hard. Did he do something with boxes? I get a sense of boxes and tape."

"He owned a shipping company."

"He is saying he is sorry over and over again," I told them. "He worked so hard. He kept long hours. He keeps saying he's sorry."

"Yes, that's right. Sometimes he worked for days at a time and didn't even come home. He was a workaholic."

"Your dad is upset about a Jenny or Janie?" I asked.

"Ginny, our mom," was the reply. "She has been very upset."

"Your father certainly did not treat himself well. He seems to be a man who was very hard on himself, always wanting to achieve. He is telling me that he wanted to be the best father possible. Which one is Adrienne?" I asked.

"That's me," said the girl on my left.

"Adrienne, your dad is sorry he wasn't able to be there for your wedding . . . to walk you down the aisle."

"I got married two weeks after he died. Daddy, we love you," shouted Adrienne.

At that point we all got very emotional. Even I could hardly hold back my tears. "He is saying something about a nut or peanut. He is talking about having a peanut. I have no idea what this means."

"Peanut was his dog. It was hit by a car and died. My father was devastated."

"Was this dog brown and white?"

"Yes, yes. He was the runt of the litter, and Dad always felt sorry for him. He used to take Peanut under his arm and carry him around."

"Your dad is going on about not being fair to himself. He says that he should have slowed down but thought his family expected this of him. He thought that as a father he was supposed to work hard and earn money for his family. He never wanted your mother or you girls to work."

Paula spoke up, "He wouldn't stop. We told him over and over again, 'Dad, please stop working so hard.' He wouldn't stop. Mom used to call him stubborn."

"Then his company went bankrupt," Adrienne added. "I don't think he was able to handle it. He was in a terrible depression for a long time. He stayed to himself and became quiet. We didn't understand what was wrong with him."

"He is carrying on about his failing everyone," I said, feeling the father's despair. "Your father did not love himself. He tells me how he was too critical. He wishes he hadn't been so hard on himself and could have appreciated life more. He wants you to know that he is beginning to learn how to love himself."

"Good!" said Paula. "We love you, Daddy."

"He spent so much time concerned with others that he didn't take time for himself," I said. "Your father is showing me a glove box . . . in a car. It's a glove compartment. I see a hand going into it. Do you understand this? This is the impression he is giving me."

❖

"Yes," the girls said. "That is where the gun was," Paula continued. "The gun that he used in the car."

All of a sudden I felt a cold metal handgun in my mouth. I sensed the trigger being pulled and the feeling of an explosion inside my head. I was stunned and had to sit still for several minutes before I could resume the reading.

"Your father wants me to tell you that he is fine now. He is very alive and is with Mums. Do you understand?"

"Mums is his mother. She died awhile ago. I'm happy she is with him," remarked Paula.

" 'She made me some apple cobbler,' says your dad."

"That was her specialty. Whenever we were sick, or if we needed cheering up, she would always make us apple cobbler. It always made things seem a little bit better," Paula acknowledged.

The moment the girls said that, I had an impression of two plates full of comforting apple pie being handed to them.

Several months after this reading, Adrienne called me about a dream she had of her father. She was with him and the dog Peanut in a park. Her father showed her a beautiful house that he had made of white marble. It had very high ceilings and lovely, spacious rooms. Her father told her the house represented the love he had found within himself. He was now treating himself like a king. And why not? He deserved it!

My Princess

When I met Anthony, I felt as if I were Jack and he was the giant. He looked down at me with probing dark brown eyes from his height of six feet five, and his closely cropped mustache gave him an almost sinister appearance. Yet he seemed unsure why he was there and kept tapping his foot nervously on the floor. As I tried to make him feel more comfortable by explaining how I worked, he just nodded his head and grunted, "Ah-huh."

Those first fifteen minutes were agonizing. I psychically sensed some health concerns he had and a potential problem at his job. He acknowledged my insights with a very meek "Ah-huh." I began to worry that this man was so emotionally vacant that it would be hard to tune in to the spirit world on his behalf.

Finally, I began to receive some spiritual impressions.

"Do you know someone named Joseph?" I asked him. "He has something to do with Philadelphia."

He grunted, "No. Well, yes."

I told him that this man was speaking about his father, at which point the silent Anthony opened his mouth and said that Joseph was his father's father. Anthony's grandfather came through with such incredible details, such as the name of the park where Anthony had played as a child, the names of his two sisters, and the circumstances of his own death. But the giant man across from me seemed only mildly moved, and clearly not very much impressed at all, until I uttered a particular name.

"Your grandfather is talking about someone named Donna. Do you understand this name?"

"Yes, yes, I do," he replied with eyebrows raised.

"Joseph wants me to tell you that he has Donna. He has Donna here for you. Donna wants to speak with you. Do you understand?"

Suddenly, Anthony began to sob uncontrollably. This stoical and serious man who just a few minutes before could not even verbalize a sentence was now crying like a

❖

child. I made sure he was comfortable, but at the same time I had to hold my concentration to keep receptive to the spirit vibrations.

"I am hearing a lady's voice now. It is kind of a singsong. She is calling out, 'Ton.' I guess it is short for Tony."

"She always called me that," Anthony blurted out. "How is she? My baby, my baby! Please tell her I'm sorry. Please tell her."

"She is alive and kicking, she says. She is a beautiful woman. I see this lady with an hourglass figure and long brown hair. She could be a model."

Anthony nodded in acknowledgment.

"She is telling me that you were always the boss. She is showing me a closetful of dresses. Now she is showing me hundreds of shoes. It's incredible! So many dresses, coats, shoes, all sorts of stuff. She is telling me that you picked out all her clothes. Is that right?"

"Yes, yes, right. I did. I bought everything for her, everything! She was my princess, and I dressed her like one," he insisted.

"She is also showing me diamonds, rubies, earrings, bracelets, all different kinds of jewelry."

"I gave her everything. There wasn't a thing in the world I didn't give her. I wanted her to be the most beautiful woman in the world!"

"Donna is telling me you wanted her to be perfect. Now she is talking about Las Vegas. About working in Las Vegas, or being in Las Vegas."

By now Anthony was completely engrossed in what he was hearing.

"Yes," he said. "We met in Las Vegas. I met her with some friends. That's right."

"She is telling me something about a prize, or a bet."

"Jesus Christ!" Anthony shouted. "How the hell would you know that?" He rubbed his eyes with his hand and slowly began to speak as if unraveling a deep, dark secret. "I . . . I won her."

"Pardon me?"

"I won her in a bet with some guys. But it's not what it sounds like. I fell in love with her. We loved each other," he said sheepishly.

I have heard many things throughout my career as a medium, but this was a first. I remember thinking to myself, *just when you think you heard it all . . .*

"It isn't how it sounds," started Anthony. "At first I thought, you know, she was just a hooker, but she was a good person. She was more than that to me. I loved her, I really did, and she loved me. It was special. We got married, but . . ."

His voice began to break. "I didn't treat her right. I was a no-good bastard." He shook his head as tears streamed down his face.

I handed him a box of tissues and tried to console him, asking him if he would like to stop the session. But he wanted to reach his "baby doll."

"Does she know I tried to get to her? Tell her please. Tell her I am sorry about the operation. Please, please tell her!"

I explained to Anthony that he could send these thoughts himself, that she would be able to hear him.

But then Donna interrupted. "She wants me to ask you about the cuff links. She is showing me gold cuff links with an anchor inscribed on each one."

"Yeah, she gave them to me for our anniversary."

"She is telling me you never wear them."

❖

"Geez, I was just looking at them yesterday. I can hardly believe it. It is so real."

"Donna is telling me that she is finding her happiness. She wants you to know that it wasn't only your fault, that it was hers as well. She tells me she should have known better. She should have known she was beautiful, but she didn't think she was."

Anthony looked up at me with his red eyes and softly spoke. "I tried to make her the way *I* wanted her to be. I was a fool. Now I have nothing."

I looked down at the floor, then heard Donna once again. "Donna is talking about going to Paris and Beverly Hills. She is showing me a mirror. I haven't a clue what this means, but she is showing me a mirror."

"That's it. I flew her there to have her operations," Anthony replied.

Mostly out of curiosity I asked, "What kind of operations?"

"For her body and her face. I knew some doctors who could make her look better, you know, change her, make her the way I wanted. So she had some procedures done."

"How many?"

"I don't know. Twenty-something. I know I should have stopped her, but she wanted to please me. She wanted to be everything I wanted. It's my fault she's dead. Please tell her I'm sorry."

I sat dumbfounded. I did not want to place my own judgments on what I had heard. As I continued, I hoped that somehow this situation could be healed.

"She knows you are sorry," I said. "She is talking about Cliff. Clifford. She doesn't want you to sue him."

"I am going to court this week. Donna was going in for a bust reduction. He overdid the anesthesia. He killed her!"

"Don't blame it on this man," I told him. "Donna is saying it was her heart. Something was wrong with her heart,
and some kind of reaction to the anesthesia."

Anthony responded, "This Clifford was the anesthetist.
He gave her the wrong medication. But I know it was really
my fault. I insisted that she have the operation done. She
did it for me. How can she ever forgive me?"

"She knows you are sorry and forgives you," I insisted.
"She is telling me that she finally thinks she is pretty. She is
saying at last she realizes that her beauty is not outside of
her. She made the mistake of not seeing her inner beauty
while she was with you. She is saying she didn't know any
better. She wants you to think about Rosarita. I think she
means Rosarita, Mexico. She is showing me some kind of a
café. You are both sitting at a small table. You're both
happy."

Anthony looked at me in amazement. "That was the
place we used to go to get away. It was a small café. We
used to talk about opening one just like it when we got
old."

I looked at Anthony. "One day you will have a café,
and you will not worry about what each other looks like.
You'll just enjoy one another and the atmosphere you have
created."

Anthony left my office a renewed soul. Through his own
tearful admission, he had experienced tremendous pain because of his petty expectations about Donna's appearance.
Instead of realizing that the love he shared with Donna was
the real beauty he sought, he tried to make her into some
kind of beautiful doll.

In the end, he was relieved that the love of his life still
existed and that she would be waiting for his arrival one
day in heaven.

❁

It Is Unbelievable!

I want to recount a wonderful experience that I had with a remarkable family. The appointment was originally set for two people, but instead five showed up. The first one through the door was Cleo Monroe, the mother. Next came daughters Jasmine and Caroline, followed by Caroline's husband, Walter. Walter wheeled in a young man about twenty years old. His name was Lenny. Lenny had muscular dystrophy and could barely speak, but it struck me somehow that he was quite spiritually evolved. Walter wheeled the chair to one side of the room, and everyone else positioned themselves on the couch and the surrounding chairs.

I really enjoyed the exuberance and candor of this family. Too often there is so much bickering and resentment among family members. After the preliminaries about my work, I sat back and began to meditate to open myself to the spirits. I could sense so much love in this family that I knew I was about to have an incredible experience.

I spied a large spirit woman to the right of Cleo, dressed in a peppermint-striped dress and a white hat. She was accompanied by a spirit man, about two inches shorter than she was, wearing a dark bluish suit with a bright baby blue tie. They greeted me with great big smiles, and I knew instantly that they were Cleo's parents, which she confirmed.

"Your mother is using the word 'Mama,' " I said.

Everybody nodded in the affirmative. Cleo answered, "Ah-huh, that's what we all called her. How is her rheumatism these days?"

We all laughed at Cleo's offhand remark.

"Mama is telling me that she loves the pretty angels in the window and that you should not give up yet; it is too early."

Caroline broke in, "See, Ma, I told you! I had a feeling we shouldn't sell yet."

"Your father is talking about not being foolish after working so hard. I think he is referring to all of you. Mama is mentioning about how she loves the angels, and she is telling me that you are helping lots of people even though you don't know it. She is telling me about the store. She loves the store."

Walter interrupted, "That's unbelievable."

"Why?" I asked.

Walter responded, "Well, we have this store that we bought with the money from Mama's will, and it's not doing too well, so we were thinking of selling it."

I asked him, "What kind of store?"

Walter looked straight at me. "An angel store. We sell angel paraphernalia."

A few moments passed, and I continued with another message. "This Mama is a real character. I like her. She has a zest for life."

"Yeah, you got that right. Mama was always the life of the party!" exclaimed Cleo.

"Your mother says you made *her* mashed potatoes last night."

Jasmine spoke up for the first time. "Yes, Mom made them for us along with Grandma's recipe for fried chicken. It was good, just like Mama made."

I then heard Mama laughing in my right ear and saying, "No way, you used too much butter!" I told all of them this, and we shared a big laugh.

"The man here, is his name Eddie? He keeps saying Eddie."

"Yes," said Walter "that was his name."

Cleo chimed in, "But we all called him Buddy. Eddie was his Christian name."

"This man gives me the impression of limping. Did he have trouble in his left leg?"

Both girls answered, "Yes!"

Jasmine added, "He was hurt in the war and had a piece of shrapnel stuck in his leg."

"He is dancing now, and he wants me to tell you that he no longer has a limp."

"Praise the Lord!" shouted Cleo.

"I have to tell you folks that you are wonderful to work with. You are so open and seem to understand exactly what the process of spirit communication is all about."

"We ought to," said Cleo. "We were all raised with it. Mama used to bring me to spiritualists ever since I was a little girl."

"And Mama used to read our tea leaves all the time!" added Jasmine.

"No wonder. Now I understand," I said.

I must remind you that all this time Lenny was sitting there in his wheelchair, unable to speak. But that didn't stop him from crying out in enthusiasm, especially when information came through that he understood. Suddenly, an unexpected spirit came through with a voice that completely startled me.

"Does anyone know the name of Ross?"

Lenny let out a piercing scream.

"Yes!" everyone cried in unison. Caroline spoke out. "He's our daddy!"

Then everyone started to speak at once: "How are you, Daddy? How are you feeling now, Daddy?" I had a difficult time concentrating on what Daddy had to say.

I should point out that, unlike the other spirits, Daddy

chose not to show his physical appearance but instead to impress me with his personality.

I described to the family what I was receiving. "This man is a bit difficult. What I mean is that he seems very stubborn and doesn't want to be bothered with anyone telling him what to do. Does this make sense?"

"Yes," shouted everyone simultaneously.

Cleo continued, "He was a pain in the ass. Weren't you, Daddy?" Ross was Cleo's husband, but like all the rest she called him Daddy.

"He thought he knew everything and that we were all crazy," she added, laughing to herself.

Cleo then began to share with me her husband's thoughts about anything spiritual.

"He never believed in any of this. He thought when you died, you were buried in the dirt and were dinner for the earthworms."

Jasmine said, "Anytime any of us would even talk about heaven, Daddy would say that if it did exist, we would all probably never see it 'cause we were all going to hell for talking so much to dead people."

"He was a Bible man," said Caroline. "He only believed what he read in that book." She continued, "His father was a preacher in Mississippi."

Lenny let out another high-pitched shriek, as if agreeing with his sister.

At that moment I was strongly impressed with the feelings of Daddy, and I began to relate them. "Did your father have trouble with his lungs before his passing? Because he gives me a condition that he can't breathe. I feel my lungs unable to fill with air," I said as I held my chest.

"He died from emphysema," Walter said.

❖

"Your father is telling me that he met someone named Libby."

"Oh, yes, that was his sister. She died about twenty years ago," replied Cleo.

"Your father says that he remembers the hospital and how hard it was to breathe. He knew he was going to die, and when he did, he awakened in a beautiful place. It was like a ward, but not like any place on earth. At first he thought he was dreaming because everything was very beautiful. He is showing me a garden of flowers, and people, and impressing me with the thought that he didn't know where he was. His sister Libby came to him, and he couldn't believe it. He thought he was going to see Jesus and the angels, but she kept saying that that was not the way it was. He says that he was seeing people he hadn't seen in years. He says he felt very real, and the place was very real to him. He then saw his mother and father. They were dressed perfectly. He is laughing now. He says his mother had white hair most of her life, but now it was brown. She also had a birthmark on her neck that was no longer there. He is telling me that he is in a wonderful place, in the country, similar to where he grew up. Everything is so serene and peaceful. He is saying that he goes fishing every day."

"We used to go fishing together all the time," interjected Walter.

"He is telling me that he is sorry for believing that life ends in the earth as he once thought. He knows now that it's all very natural for life to continue after we leave our bodies. He wants to say he is sorry for not believing you when you talked to him about the spiritual side of life. He knows better now. It is definitely not what he had expected."

"That's all right, Daddy, we love you," replied Caroline.

The rest of the family called out in agreement, including Lenny.

Then Ross addressed his son Lenny with a special, profoundly touching message. He told him, "You were put on this earth with a debilitating disease in order to teach people around you about unconditional love."

With that, the whole family declared, "Alleluia!"

The loving acceptance in Ross's message—and indeed, the close-knit warmth of the Monroe family—is precious and rare. Like Anthony, we expect perfection in the outside world, or like Carl, we demand it of ourselves. Perhaps we learned it from our parents or teachers, who criticized us so much that we strove to be perfect at any cost to please them. Perfectionism is a curse.

Ultimately, life can never be fully gratifying or appreciated if we don't become aware of our own inner power, our connection to the God Force energy. To do that, we have to let go of expectations and live the life destined for our own uniqueness. Peace comes only when we are true to our soul's nature.

9

✻

Guilt

We suffer primarily not from our vices or our weaknesses, but from our illusions. We are haunted, not by reality, but by those images we have put in place of reality.

—Daniel J. Boorstin

I have often heard people say, "A little guilt is good for the soul," but I disagree. I'm not talking about genuine remorse about a wrongdoing for which we can make amends. I mean the kind of self-punishing guilt that goes hand in hand with feelings of low self-esteem and inadequacy.

Often, we feel guilty because of some sort of self-imposed expectation of how we should or should not behave. Usually we base such an expectation on fear. We say or do something out of fear because we think the truth cannot be told. Later, we regret our lies and blunders, and feel guilty over making such mistakes. In our hearts we feel we have sinned and must be punished.

Any form of self-condemnation is not good for the soul. Guilt not only creates disharmony in the spiritual and emotional bodies, but also can be related to many of the health ailments from which we suffer, as you will see from the following readings.

I Think I Killed Her

The following session was done at my home in 1995. At the time I was just becoming recognized by television audiences from *The Joan Rivers Show* and the NBC show *The Other Side*. A woman saw me on TV and wrote me a letter begging for a reading. As she said, "My life is in ruin, and I cannot go on."

Dana was about five foot seven and overweight. When she walked in, I felt her burden of despair and depression. There was a heaviness in the air.

Dana gave me a charming "Good morning" in a light Southern accent, and she thanked me profusely for giving her a session. "Your assistant called and said there had been a cancellation," she told me. "It's a sign from heaven because today is my daddy's birthday!"

I told her that the spirit world works in very mysterious ways when it wants to be known. She smiled as if she knew something I didn't. We sat down together, and I began my prayer.

It took about a half hour until Elsie came through, the spirit that I could tell Dana was waiting for.

"I have a lady here with a beautiful floral-patterned dress. She has a very soft complexion and has brown hair pulled back toward the top of her head. She is telling me that she has a full head of hair now, not just strands!"

With that information Dana pulled out some tissues to wipe the tears from her eyes.

"That's Mom. Is she okay?" she asked softly.

"Yes, she says. Made it through okay. She is telling me about the scar. A scar near her lip. Is that correct?"

Dana shook her head. "I honestly don't remember. Why would she say something like that?"

"A form of identity. My guides always insist that spirits give information to verify their presence."

Dana picked up her handbag and began to fidget inside. A few moments later, she pulled out a picture and looked at it.

"Wow, yeah, you're right. There is a small scar near the bottom lip. You can see for yourself." She showed me the photo, and sure enough, there was the scar.

"Your mother is talking about someone by the name of Stella. Is she someone you know?" I asked.

"Yes, that is my sister."

"Are you not speaking to your sister? Your mother is telling me that you have had a fight. Is there someone with the name of Paul as well?"

Dana could not believe her ears. She looked at me in wonder.

"Yes, that's my brother, Paulie. Yeah, we had a fight. Oh, my God. What is she saying? Please help me, Mom."

"Your mother is showing me some sort of legal paper. I don't know what this means, but I am feeling that it has something to do with a court. She gives me this feeling of a trial or court hearing."

"Go on," she said. "I understand."

"She is saying that no good will come of it. You must tell them that no good will come of it, and it is wrong to behave like this."

"They will never believe this. How can I get them to believe this?" Dana asked.

"Play them the tape of this session," I responded.

My remark didn't seem to change her attitude, and Dana remained perplexed.

"Your mom wants you to know that she is with Marty. Do you understand that name?"

Dana started to cry once again. "Yes, happy birthday, Daddy."

"I feel this man smoked and had problems breathing."

"Yes, he died of emphysema. Is he all right?"

"Yes, he is fine. He is taking care of your mother and is with someone else. Sounds like Don."

Dana nodded affirmatively. "Yes, Donnie, his brother. He died a month ago."

At that moment the session took a dramatic turn.

"Your mother is showing me a scene of you kneeling at her bedside, and you're reciting the rosary."

"Yes, yes," Dana cried. "I prayed for her every day. I wanted her pain to stop. All she did was moan in agony. I had to help. I prayed for help. I hope I did the right thing, Mom."

I continued with my impressions, trying to give them as correctly as I could.

"Was your mother in a coma?" I asked.

"Yes," acknowledged Dana through tears. "She had a stroke. She couldn't breathe on her own. They put her on machines. I couldn't stand seeing her like that."

I couldn't believe what I said next:

"Your mother is telling me that you pulled the tube out of her throat."

Dana was trembling. She looked down at her feet. "Yes . . . yes, I did. I didn't mean to kill her. I just couldn't stand to see her in such pain."

I was shocked. Although I am used to hearing many

❖

things in this sort of work, I am only human. I have to be very objective, and it isn't always easy.

I felt this girl's pain. After a moment I continued transmitting the mother's message.

"Your mother says it doesn't matter. She is telling me you had courage. It was an act of love. She wants you to understand that you did this because of love. She says that she left in God's time."

Still staring down at her shoes, Dana asked, "Did I kill her?"

"Your mother tells me it was out of your hands. She is saying that she remained alive anyway."

I leaned over and touched Dana's cheek and raised her head. "Your mother didn't die right away, did she?"

Dana shook her head. "No. She lasted for another week. The doctors said her heart was too weak to work anymore. It finally gave out."

I asked her, "Then why are you putting yourself through this? You didn't kill her. She went naturally."

"Because Paulie and Stella have accused me of killing her. They are taking me to court. I really don't know if I can handle any more."

I sat for about five minutes and said nothing. Suddenly I felt a tap on my shoulder. It was Dana's father, Marty. He impressed me with a name of someone.

I leaned over and asked Dana, "Do you know the name of Simon?"

She gave me a queer sort of look. "That is so strange. Why are you asking me that? I have a meeting this afternoon with him. He is a lawyer. A friend of mine recommended him."

"Your father wants me to tell you that this Simon is

going to help you, and you will be fine. Your dad said this Simon was heavenly appointed."

With this last bit of information Dana perked up. I could tell by the brightness of her eyes that this girl, who had been ostracized by her family and had condemned herself to hell, at last had been given something to live for. Finally, she had been shown the light.

A few months later, Dana called my office to thank me and let me know that Simon indeed had helped her. The case had been dropped, and she was in the midst of reconciling with her family. She wanted me to know that she also had lost thirty pounds and was dating once again.

A Well-Kept Secret

When Robin, a young lady around twenty-five, came to see me, I wondered, *Why is she here? She is too young to have lost anyone.* I was doing the very thing I tell my students not to do—I was rationalizing. I recited my prayer, and the reading commenced, but shortly after, I got a funny feeling:

"This is very weird, but I want to sing the song 'Ring Around the Rosy.' I am seeing two blond-haired girls dressed the same and playing. They are singing this song."

Immediately, Robin confirmed that it made sense to her.

"I am being impressed with a lady. She is telling me you both have the same color eyes and hair. Do you understand this?"

"Yes, I totally understand, James," she said.

"I feel like I want to say the name Rachel. She is telling me Rachel. She is very close to you. Very close. I don't know why, but you have such a strong connection. I feel like you are almost the same."

❖

Robin answered in a high-pitched voice. "She is my twin sister, Rachel. She died several years ago."

"Twins! No wonder I feel that she is so close to you. Your sister is showing me a nice house on top of a hill. She is talking about moving. Did you just buy a house? And something about a blue bird or bluejay. Do you understand this?"

Robin suddenly blurted out, "Bluebird Lane! That is the street the house is on."

We both shook our heads. "Wow!" I exclaimed.

And she said, "Unbelievable!"

"Your sister wants me to tell you that she has been around you a lot. Have you felt her?"

"No, not really. I have had some dreams, though."

"Dreams are a way in which the spirit communicates, but I think your sister means that she has been watching you."

Robin sighed, "Oh, that's great! I love that!"

"She has seen you picking out wallpaper. She liked the yellow one with the small flowers."

I looked at Robin; her reaction was one of amazement.

"Oh, my God. I was just looking at it. I actually bought the one she is speaking about. Oh, my God."

I replied, "She was trying to impress you to buy it. She is telling me that she knew you received the thought because you then thought about her."

"That's right. I held it up and wondered if Rachel would have liked it."

As Robin was finishing her sentence, I suddenly felt a wave of emotion overcome me. I felt as though I was about to cry, and I had to share what I was feeling.

"Your sister loves you very much, and she wants me to convey to you that she had to go. But she wants to hang around and enjoy the physical life through you. Is it okay if she tags around from time to time?"

Robin began to get teary-eyed herself. She looked at the ceiling and spoke to her sister, "Anytime, Rach . . . I love you."

At this point I experienced an odd sensation. Here was a young woman sitting in front of me, giving such loving emotion to her identical sister who was standing to the other side of me. The two sounded exactly alike, so it seemed that one person was holding both sides of the conversation.

Robin then shouted "Please tell her I am sorry!"

I stared at Robin, waiting to hear her sister's reply.

"She is not acknowledging you. But hold on . . . Was there something wrong with her blood? She is showing me blood cells being attacked. It feels like her bone marrow. Did she have leukemia?" I asked.

Robin started to cry. "Yes, she did."

"She is telling me that you donated blood for her. You thought you could save her life."

"Silly of me, wasn't it?"

I responded, "No, why do you say that? It was a beautiful gesture. Your sister will never forget your act of kindness. She will always feel indebted to you."

Robin shook her head and then broke down. "But it didn't work. She died. We were best friends. I miss her so much . . . It was all my fault! I jinx people!"

I spent the next ten minutes calming Robin. She regained her composure and seemed fine.

"Robin, your sister tells me that it was not your fault she died. It was her natural time to go. She is telling me you must try to understand none of it was your fault."

Robin just sat there staring right through me.

❈

Rachel then impressed me with some unexpected news. "Do you know the name Jake?"

Robin looked down for a few seconds and then replied, "What did you say? Did you say Jake?"

"Yes, Jake. Your sister is giving me that name."

Robin looked horrified and put her face in her hands.

"She wants you to know that Jake is okay. Jake is back already. It wasn't his turn yet, and you weren't ready. It wasn't a sin! Your sister wants me to tell you it wasn't a sin!"

Robin was half in shock and half in disbelief.

"She doesn't want you to feel guilty. She wants you to love yourself! You were not to blame. Please love yourself!"

Since I didn't understand what was going on, I was hoping that it made sense to Robin. When I looked at her face, I knew the message had hit home.

I said softly, "You are safe and very loved."

After a few moments of silence Robin slowly began to unravel the mysteriousness of her sister's communication.

"When I was sixteen I got pregnant, and my sister and I used to pretend the baby's name was Jake. We would never say the word pregnant; we'd just say Jake. After a month or so into the pregnancy, my boyfriend left me, and I had no choice but to get an abortion. My sister was the only one who knew. She promised me that she would never tell anyone. It was our secret."

Robin dropped her head to her chest, and tears flowed. In between sobs she mentioned that soon after that her sister developed leukemia and died.

"I always felt guilty for Rachel's death. I thought God was punishing me for what I had done to Jake."

Robin's story was very touching, and I was deeply moved by this young woman's anguish and feelings of devastating guilt. I explained at length that God is not a vengeful God.

"God doesn't punish us," I said. "Only we punish ourselves."

I reassured her that the soul never dies and is never in physical pain.

I reminded Robin of what her sister said. "Jake has come back and is experiencing life elsewhere on earth."

After several minutes Robin wiped away her tears and looked at the ceiling as if she was saying a silent prayer to her sister. Then she began to thank me.

"I have been living in torture for so many years. I really did believe I was responsible for Rachel's death."

Robin left my office with a light heart and a new sense of herself. She had felt the compassionate love of a sister, and had the reassurance that Rachel was not only looking out for her, but would continue to share in many important parts of her life. They were twins bound together forever, and not even death could keep them apart.

The Gunshot

One Saturday night, a week before Christmas, a married couple who had attended several of my public demonstrations invited me to their Pasadena, California, living room to meet six complete strangers. There were four women and two men. I wasn't sure if anyone knew each other very well, and I didn't even know if they knew what to expect from me. However, each guest showed a willingness to open his or her heart to face the pain and grief hidden inside. I explained how I worked, and began with my prayer. In the first half of the session I read for three people. The

❖

young couple's grandparents came through with some messages about their financial situation. An aunt revealed herself to one woman by giving proof that the woman had three job changes in the past year. The communication included a potpourri of details, about everything from stomach ulcers to going camping. The evidential information was quite extraordinary. As I observed the reactions of the group, most appeared quite satisfied, except for a single man named Rob.

During a break time, as I left the room, I overheard Rob say, "He has to be making it up. You know, he asks all those questions. Some of the stuff was so general, anyone could do it."

As I turned back toward him, I noticed my skeptic's face turn red as he struggled to shove a chip down his throat. I decided not to say anything at that time, and instead just sighed and looked up to heaven.

Fifteen minutes later, when I started the session with a prayer, I was almost instantly directed toward Rob.

"May I come to you?" I gestured at Rob.

Rob had a blank look on his face. Then he smiled and said, "Sure, let 'em rip."

I could tell Rob was very uncomfortable and was trying his best to play along. I believe that he was trying to find some gimmick behind it all. When people resist the work that I do, I have to concentrate all the more on maintaining the spiritual vibration to receive impressions.

I immediately had the sensation that there was a man standing right behind him. As I focused my energy, I began to see the man more clearly. He had sandy hair, green eyes, and a charming smile. His hands were atop Rob's shoulders.

"Are you familiar with Akron, Ohio?"

❁

Rob's face turned white. He looked at all the others in disbelief. I think he was hoping that they would say something to ease his discomfort. Then he looked at me.

"Yeah, I grew up there before my dad was transferred."

"Do you remember St. Lucy's church or school?"

"Yes. Yeah . . . How the hell . . ."

Rob began to shake and stammer. "Who is it? Who's talking to you?" Rob's solid exterior was beginning to crumble.

I continued with my impressions.

"I have a gentleman here who says he knows you. He says he lived in Akron."

Rob interjected, "Is it my grandfather? He lived there. In fact, he was born and raised there." His nervousness was now very evident in his speech.

"This man is speaking of a gun," I said.

"My grandfather had a gun. It was a shotgun. He used to teach me how to use it."

I knew from the vibration that the spirit standing behind Rob was not his grandfather. I sent mental thoughts to the spirit and asked it to tell me who he was. By now Rob was squirming in his seat, and his apprehensive energy seemed to spread throughout the room. Everyone was sitting on pins and needles, waiting to hear who this mystery guest was.

"He is someone you have not seen in years. He is telling me that you would remember him by something or someone named Spike."

Rob's eyes opened wide in agitation. He could not stop shaking. "Jesus Christ . . . Jesus Christ, it can't be . . . It can't be. Danny? Danny, is that you?"

Suddenly, tears started to well up in Rob's eyes. "Spike is his bike. He used to refer to his bike as Spike. It was a joke between us."

❖

"He lived down the street, he says."

"Yes, I know, It's Danny Timmons. We grew up together."

Then Rob, perhaps in shock, stood up and pointed his finger at me and yelled. "Who are you? Is this some kind of cruel joke? Someone told you. Someone had to tell you."

I waited several minutes for him to quiet down, and the other people in the room urged Rob to calm down and relax.

Rob collapsed into the chair and held his face in his hands. I reminded Rob that no one in the room knew this information, and assured him that I was genuine. I think my words comforted him somewhat, and this little bit of re-assurance helped him to feel that he could trust me.

"Danny is showing me a gun. It is the same gun I saw before. Do you understand this?"

"Yes . . . yes, I understand," Rob mumbled.

He mumbled something else to himself, and I asked him to speak a little louder.

Rob raised his voice and said, "I have a message for Danny. Tell him I am sorry. I really am sorry. I have been trying my whole life to make it up to you, Danny. Please forgive me. I stop by the cemetery every time I go back home for a visit. It's right across the street from St. Lucy's, where we went to school. I wished it didn't happen. I hit myself every day because of it."

"Danny knows you didn't mean it. He wants to thank you for all the loving thoughts and work you have done in his name. He says it's now time to let go of the guilt. It's holding you back from opening your heart. He wants you to live the life you truly want. He wants you to be happy."

Afterward, we learned that Rob and Danny had been neighborhood friends. One day Rob suggested that they play cowboys and Indians, and he got his grandfather's shotgun. As they were playing, the gun accidentally went off, and the shot pierced Danny's chest, killing him instantly. Needless to say, Rob's life was never the same again. From the age of eight Rob had carried the guilt of Danny's death with him. The memory of watching his young friend die in front of his eyes haunted him endlessly. He could never get away from the images and feelings it stirred. The guilt of the accident pushed Rob to become a doctor. As a surgeon Rob spends fourteen-hour days saving people's lives. The guilt may have benefited other people, but it was time for Rob finally to lay it to rest.

As these stories illustrate, the terrible burden of regret for events that we cannot change can destroy lives and weigh us down heavily on our spiritual journey. When we carry around the burden of guilt, we stay focused in the past. The past is over, and there is nothing we can do to bring it back. One of the great spiritual truths that I have learned over these many years is that our personal power exists only in the here and now.

The best way to release guilt is to forgive ourselves and others, and to remind ourselves that as spiritual beings we are on an eternal journey. We are here to learn and grow from all our experiences.

IO

❖

Fear

What do you have to fear? Nothing. Whom do you
have to fear? No one. Why? Because whoever has
joined forces with God obtains three great privileges:
omnipotence without power, intoxication without
wine, and life without death.

—St. Francis of Assisi

J ust as love is the great unifying force, fear is the great
dividing one. While the soul possesses an accumulation
of past-life experiences and karmic obligations in its
memory, the personality arrives in this world a blank slate.
Its identity is developed and shaped by the people and the
environment in which it resides. As we grow, we define ourselves based on the judgments and beliefs of others. Gradu-
ally, if we begin to fall into the trap of the lower nature and
forget our true loving selves, we may become fearful.

Fear is a deceptive creation of our minds. It is not real.
Yes, there are very real things to be afraid of out there in the
world, but I'm not talking about the fear that comes with
our basic survival instincts. I'm referring to emotional fears
that come from faulty impressions and illusions. We have

been so programmed by world events and violence that we believe the world is a fearful place. We grow afraid of things or people we think are out to get us. We attempt to live up to other people's standards, and become something that we're not. In essence, we are not being true to ourselves.

When our minds become encased in fear, we often experience it physically. Our physical bodies tense as we replay a fearful situation over and over in our minds and scare ourselves further. Then our energy becomes weakened. Sometimes, we feel that we literally just can't move and find ourselves dreading the future.

When fear enters a person's life, she shuts out the light of the soul. Any ray of truth that may be trying to alleviate the fear can't get through. When we succumb to our fears, they inevitably take charge of our lives and hold us back from taking chances and doing the things we want.

So, how can you overcome and control fear? First, by thinking positively and using the universal law of affinity, "like attracts like." Whenever a negative or fearful thought comes into mind, I repeat the following affirmation: "Healthy am I, happy am I, holy am I." I let it sink into my subconscious. As I have said many times, you create your destiny by how you think. By replacing a negative with a positive, you begin to attract assurance and trust rather than fear and uncertainty. Second, we can control fear by using the law of cause and effect constructively. If you want good in your life, you have to be loving and kind in the situations you encounter. You cannot expect peace and contentment if you're creating misery for others. Last, if you want happiness and joy, you can't look to the world outside you for the truth. When you dwell in the higher God

❖

consciousness, you will always come from a place of love and feel that love inside.

∽✺∾

Remember God always says yes; we say no.

∽✺∾

The following readings demonstrate how fearful thinking incapacitates people.

I'm Afraid

Several years ago a couple came to see me looking rather peaked. Like many people, the woman, Mira, was a bit anxious about having a communication from the spirit world. Her husband, Lloyd, seemed rather somber. He had a long, drawn expression on his face and dark, piercing eyes. Mira explained that they were afraid to let their family know about their visit because they didn't want to be judged as weird or strange. I told them that I understood their concerns, and reassured them that nothing strange or weird was about to happen.

As I began the séance, I quickly felt a strong, cold sensation on Mira's left side. I closed my eyes and saw a woman standing there.

"There is a lady on your left side, Mira. She goes by the name of Sari or Sarah. Do you understand the name?"

Mira was in shock. She opened her mouth, but nothing came out. She looked over at Lloyd, and he assured her that it was all right for her to speak.

"Yes, sir. I know that name."

❖

"This Sarah is telling me that she is associated with your mother and is one of three."

"Yes, she is my mother's sister, one of three siblings— my mother, Aunt Sarah, and their brother."

I could see Sarah's spirit only from her torso up. Many times spirits will not show their complete self to me, and sometimes I see just a face.

"Sarah is telling me something about Franklin Street. Do you understand this?" I asked Mira.

After a few moments she replied, "Yes, that is the street she used to live on."

"She is rubbing her left arm. It appears to be discolored like a burn from her elbow to her hand. She is telling me it is all better now."

Mira spoke up. "Oh, my goodness, yes. When I was a little girl, I visited my aunt at her house on Franklin Street. She was preparing tea, and as she picked the kettle off the stove it slipped, and the water scalded her arm very badly. I remember that incident very well because she had that scar her whole life."

"I never knew that," said Lloyd.

I then turned to Lloyd and told him that the lady was very happy that he was taking such good care of her daughter.

"Lloyd, this lady wants me to tell you that your prayers have been answered."

He gave me a puzzled look and said, "What?"

"Sarah is telling me that there is someone who wants to know why you didn't bring his baseball glove today like you were planning."

Lloyd and Mira looked at each other and started to cry.

Mira muttered, "Oh, my God . . . is it him?"

"This is the little boy you lost. He tells me that he died in

✿

his hospital room. He is speaking very fast. He says he had bad blood."

"Yes, he had leukemia," Lloyd responded.

"He wants you to know that he is okay, and that Granny B was at the hospital, too. Do you understand this?"

Through his tears Lloyd said, "Yes, that is my mother. He called Mira's mother Granny A and my mother Granny B. My mother died a year before our Joshua."

"Is he all right, then?" asked Mira.

"Yes, quite fine. He is telling me that he was very scared of dying. He says that he didn't want to fall into the dark hole. Does that make sense?" I asked.

"Yes," said Mira. "A month before he died he had dreams that he fell into a black hole and was eaten by some sort of monster."

"He is telling me that he was afraid that when he died, he wouldn't be able to see you or Mr. Big Foot or Cottonball again. I don't know what this means."

"They were his pets. Mr. Big Foot is a German shepherd, and Cottonball is his rabbit."

"He says Whiskers is with him."

"That was his other rabbit that died."

"Sarah is saying that Joshua is with a lot of animals."

I continued. "Your son feels silly now for being so afraid. He says he comes to see you all the time. He wants you to know that he has played the game that Dad promised. Do you understand?"

Lloyd explained that he made a promise to play a game of baseball with his son after he got out of the hospital.

"Oh, now I understand what he means by the baseball glove," I said.

Joshua then began to speak very quickly once again, and as I listened, I began to laugh.

"Your boy wants to tell you that he is very happy. He says that it is like living in Candyland over there."

Mira smiled. "He used to play it all the time!"

Sarah reassured the couple that little Joshua was extremely happy.

I told them, "He now knows there is nothing ever to be afraid of."

What's Out There?

Not long ago I had a very unusual reading and felt it particularly apropos for the topic of fear.

Bridget was a sweet, tall young woman with flowing red hair. She had a wonderfully clean and nurturing aura, and I asked her if she was a healer of some kind. "Yes," she replied, "I'm a massage therapist." Bridget explained that she wanted a job that would enable her to help people. She then told me that she had driven two hours from San Diego because her visit was an urgent one. I soon learned why.

Behind my right ear I began to hear a piercing female voice screaming at me. It was very disturbing, so I instructed my guides to let this woman know that I could hear her.

"I'm free! I'm free!" she said over and over.

"This lady is telling me that she is in the light. She says she lives in the light and no longer needs to hide. She is giving me the name of Vicky or Victoria."

"That's my mother. Her name is Victoria Jane." Bridget looked pleased. I knew this was the reason she came to see me. "Is she all right?"

"Yes, she is fine. Your mother is telling me that she has found herself again in a land of happiness and peace. She

❧

says that she understands clearly now and is no longer afraid."

Bridget had a wide grin on her soft face.

"She is telling me that she used to be afraid of everything and everyone."

Suddenly, I felt a very strange sensation and didn't understand what was happening to me. I closed my eyes, and as if being taken over, I began to feel as though I was enclosed in a box. The space around me was pitch black. I was very restricted and extremely uncomfortable, almost like being buried alive. I knew I had to break away from this sensation immediately, and so I quickly opened my eyes.

"Are you all right, James?" Bridget asked.

"I think so. That was very weird. I've never felt like that before. God, it was strange, as though I was trapped and couldn't get out."

I had a sip of water and mentally asked my spirit guides to tell me what was happening. They explained that the sensation I had felt was necessary for the communication because that is what the departed spirit felt like most of her life.

I asked, "Was your mother confined in some way?"

"Why do you say that?" she responded.

"I felt as though I was shut in a dark hole and scared to death. I don't know what it means, but that was the feeling."

Bridget looked down at her feet, then back up at me.

"My mother was agoraphobic. She would never leave the house. She was so afraid there was something outside that was going to get her. She spent much of her life inside."

Tears began rolling down Bridget's cheeks. I sat there dumbfounded.

Then I heard her mother's sweet voice and relayed the message to Bridget:

"I can walk in the sunshine now. I have met all types of people. It feels so good to be alive!"

Bridget was overjoyed at her mother's newfound freedom.

"She is saying that she now realizes that her fear caused her to miss out on a lot of experiences and that golden opportunities passed her by."

"Yes, I would say so. She didn't leave the house at all for ten years."

It was hard to believe that people could be so afraid of life. Yet I had to remember to pay attention to the communication and not get caught up in the emotional aspect; otherwise, I would not be sensitive to hearing the messages.

Then I felt a sudden pain in my chest and saw a vision of a staircase. I asked Bridget if this meant anything.

"Yes," she answered. "Mom died of a heart attack and fell on the stairs."

"Your mother wants me to tell you that she is not in pain anymore. In fact, she feels as fresh as a daisy. She is with Alfred."

"That is my grandfather, her father."

Then when I thought we were coming to the end, Victoria revealed something quite incredible. I kept looking at her standing next to Bridget, and acknowledged her messages by nodding my head and repeating, "I see," over and over. When she was finished transmitting her thoughts, I said:

"I don't know how to say this, but your mother thinks it

is important for you to know. She has found out the reason why she was always afraid to leave the house."

Bridget was amazed. "Why?"

"Your mother was showing me pictures as she was sending her thoughts. Apparently in a previous lifetime, her father was a ruler or nobleman of some sort, and she was a little girl who lived in a castle. Her mother warned her never to leave the castle because of the people who didn't like her father. She was told that if she ever left the safety of the castle, someone might take her away and never bring her back. Being curious, one day she went outside the castle walls and was immediately snatched away by men on horseback."

"Oh, my God, what happened to her?" asked Bridget.

I described the scene that her mother impressed upon me. I saw a little blond-haired girl alongside a riverbank, her throat slashed from ear to ear.

We were both stunned at the detail of Victoria's description. With this new information Bridget understood completely why her mother had been agoraphobic. I explained further that souls return to earth with certain memories deeply embedded in their spiritual body. Sometimes these experiences are traumatic and frightful like Victoria's. Many times souls try to work through these phobias and fears from a prior lifetime. Sometimes they succeed, and sometimes they do not.

Bridget thanked her mother for her love and guidance. Her mother responded by conveying one last picture. She was dressed in a free-flowing pink gown and standing in a rose garden. She was holding a white rose to her lips and blowing the petals toward her daughter.

❖

God's Wrath

I chose the following reading because it reflects an all-too-common situation—when ignorance, prejudice, and fear alienate family members and create shame, bitterness, and guilt.

Joe and Carrie, brother and sister, arrived for their appointment on a bright Wednesday afternoon. They told me they didn't believe in mediums but felt compelled to see me after having numerous dreams about a brother who had passed over. We sat for a few minutes chatting, until I suddenly became aware of a young man speaking to me.

"I have a guy here. He seems to be in his twenties. He has brown hair that is thinning, and I have a sense that he was concerned about losing it. Does that make sense?"

Carrie was dumbstruck. Joe answered, "Yes, sir, it does."

"He wants me to tell you that he awakened with a full head of hair."

"He lost all his hair right before he died," mouthed Carrie.

I looked over to Joe and said, "Joe, your brother is happy to see you here. He never expected it, but wants you to know that he truly appreciates your coming, and wants you to know that he loves you."

Joe turned red and started to tear up.

"Who is Tommy?" I asked.

"That's his name," said Joe.

"Well, Tommy is okay. He wants you to know that he has made it," I told them.

"Please tell him I'm sorry. I just couldn't ..." Joe whispered.

"Tommy wants you to know he is fine. He keeps on

showing me a Bible. He keeps pushing it toward me. Why is this?"

"Well, our mother is Evangelical, and she reads the Bible all the time. She—" Carrie's voice broke off. Then she continued, "She said Tommy would go to hell because of his lifestyle. Mom would pray for the redemption of his soul night and day."

After a few moments Carrie asked meekly, "Is my brother in hell?"

I found myself sitting stoned-faced, amazed once again about how people impose their fears on one another. After a few minutes, I gave them a message from their brother.

"Tommy wants me to tell you that he must be in heaven because he has never seen any place so beautiful and loving. He says he hasn't seen anything that resembles a place like hell. Hmm . . . he is saying that hell is on earth."

Joe piped up, "I agree."

"Your brother is telling me that he was so scared before he died because there was a part of him that still believed your mother and her religious convictions. He was in a lot of emotional turmoil. Did he die of AIDS?"

"Yes," answered Carrie.

"He says he believed your mother when she said his illness was God's punishment because he was gay. I don't feel your brother possessed a lot of self-love and self-confidence."

"Tommy was a good person," replied Carrie. "But he always felt that there was something wrong with him because of how our mother felt."

"Sexuality has nothing to do with how much love and kindness a person has in his heart. Please try to understand that. Being gay is not wrong. God knows only love.

Humans are the ones who place conditions on love, not God."

I continued to convey their brother's thoughts.

"Tommy is telling me that he loves himself more now than ever before."

"Would you please tell him that I'm sorry I didn't see him?" said Joe.

"How long did you stay away?" I asked.

"Five years. I sort of disowned him when I found out that he was gay. I was afraid that if I was around him, I would get AIDS too. I was stupid." Joe began weeping.

I sat there and felt all the repressed anger and upset Joe felt for himself. I told him not to be so hard on himself.

"One day you will understand," I said. As I was talking to Joe, Tommy interrupted.

"Joe, do you understand what he means by crossroads?"

"Yeah. That is an AIDS group I volunteer for. I started after Tommy died."

I was taken aback by Joe's complete turnaround.

"Tommy is smiling because he is very proud of you. You have touched his heart. You not only have demonstrated your love for him but also your acceptance and your willingness to learn."

Carrie reached out and grabbed Joe's hand.

"Does Tommy know I have been praying for him?" she asked.

"Yes. He is saying that he tried to thank you in a dream, but you didn't understand. He says that it had something to do with a bird."

"Huh. Yes, that's right. I had a dream three nights ago about a white dove that followed me everywhere. I had a feeling it might be Tommy," Carrie answered.

"Your brother wants you to please tell your mom that he is in heaven with Wendy," I continued.

"Wendy was Mom's good friend. What a surprise!" Carrie replied.

"Tommy says that it is much easier for him to understand life now because he sees things in a more expanded way than he did on earth."

I let both Joe and Carrie know how much their brother loved them and how he would be with them more than ever before. Before I broke off communication, Joe asked me to say one more thing to his brother.

"Could you please tell him that we love him and miss him?"

I listened for Tommy's response. "He knows, and says he will always love you. He wants me to tell you that you will all be together again one day in heaven, a place where love never dies."

So many spirits have come through, such as Joshua and Tommy, who have such a scary picture of the process of death. In Tommy's case, his fear of death was brought about by his mother's belief in a wrathful and vengeful God. In all my experiences, not one spirit has said that God was waiting on the other side to punish it for earthly deeds. I often say at my demonstrations, "If you're going to believe in something, make sure it is based on love and respect." There are far too many unhappy people who live in fear of hell, fire, and damnation.

As the reading with Victoria revealed, when fear has a paralyzing effect on our lives, it becomes impossible to realize our dreams and fulfill our potential. In such instances there are many healers, teachers, and health professionals, like Bridget, who want to help others release their pain. God's love comes through every individual on this planet. We need only to ask for help, and there are persons ready to encourage us to face our fears and to live productive lives.

11

❈

Forgiveness

We cannot love unless we have accepted forgiveness, and the deeper our experience of forgiveness is, the greater is our love.

—Paul Tillich

When I was a child, my mother used to place Band-Aids on my cuts, and then like clockwork would take them off two days later. I could never understand why she did that, since the cuts hadn't completely healed. When I asked her about it, she told me: "You must open the wound to the air so it can heal faster." The same is true of our emotional wounds, which we must expose a little to let the healing process begin.

When someone says or does something that is hurtful, we tend to hold on to the hurt and harbor ill will toward the person. From the standpoint of psychic energy, this is a mistake. Carrying an emotional hurt encourages and feeds the negative thoughts and feelings we have about it, and this sense of hurt permeates our space. As I have said many times, like attracts like. Therefore, we will attract similar elements of equal negativity to ourselves. The sooner we allow ourselves to go through the feelings of anger and frustration when hurt, the sooner we can let our pain go. And with letting go comes the true healing step: forgiveness.

What creates this power to heal oneself? What gives a person the courage to forgive? Two vital ingredients are necessary: (1) spiritual understanding that comes from a life of self-awareness, and (2) the artful practice of letting go. Compassionate persons learn the lessons of forgiveness. They realize that holding on to injury causes them to relive the pain over and over again. Forgiveness brings healing first to self and in turn helps to spread this consciousness to all humankind.

Lady, I Forgive You

The following communication is one of the sweetest examples of forgiveness I've seen. It occurred quite unexpectedly, since the spirit was someone not even related to anyone in the room. It goes to show that if there is a strong enough need, the spirit world may open up to us.

I was conducting a demonstration in front of a group of five hundred people one hot summer Saturday evening. People had waited in line for two hours before the doors opened just to get a good seat. (This activity always baffles me. Spirit finds the right individuals no matter where they sit.) In the midst of my introduction, I saw a spirit appear suddenly in the back of the room. It began floating down the center aisle. As it moved closer, I saw that it was a beautiful little girl in a dazzling yellow dress who was skipping rope. Her hair was bright blond and pulled back in two long pigtails. She stopped and stood in front of me; I could tell she was on a mission. I acknowledged her and immediately began to share my image with the audience, asking:

"Does anyone understand or recognize this little girl?"

No one raised a hand for about three minutes. I sent out a mental message to the girl to give me something stronger to go on.

She sent back a thought. "I want to talk to the lady who saw me playing. She was on her way home."

I repeated what she told me and was still searching the audience when the little girl sent me a loud and clear message:

"The lady drives a white car."

A woman stood up in the fourth row on my left side. She seemed to be a little unsure.

I asked her, "Do you know who this girl is?"

"Yes. I think I do," she replied.

Then the woman mumbled something else under her breath that no one, including myself, understood.

"Could you please speak up?" I asked.

She sadly replied, "Yes, I know who she is. I hit her with my car three years ago and killed her."

There was a loud gasp in the audience. No one expected to hear anything like that.

The woman began to cry as she continued her story.

"I was coming home from work. I turned a corner, and she came out into the street skipping rope right in front of my car. I didn't see her until it was too late. I had no time to stop."

I proceeded to carry on a dialogue with this woman based on the thoughts and impressions that I received from the little girl.

"She is showing me a stuffed animal. It is a little lamb.

She is giving me the impression that you gave this to her. Does this make sense?"

"Yes. I put one on her grave. I still go to see her all the time. I don't know what else to do," she replied.

"This little girl is showing me two boys about five or six years old around you. Do you know them?"

"No, I don't know. I don't think so."

"Who is Freddie?"

"That is my grandson. Oh, my God, Freddie and Bryan, my grandchildren. I have two grandsons ages six and seven, and the youngest is Freddie. That's right."

"This little girl is telling me that Freddie likes the game with the monkeys. Something with a barrel. What is it, please?"

An audience member came quickly to my rescue with the name Barrel of Monkeys.

"Yes, Barrel of Monkeys. That is what the girl is saying."

The woman was even more astonished. "I was with Freddie this afternoon. I was taking care of him, and all Freddie did the entire time was play with the Barrel of Monkeys. Incredible!"

"This little girl is watching you. She says that she forgives you. Do you understand that?"

The woman was a bit disconcerted by this comment.

"She came here to tell you that she forgives you, but you have to forgive yourself. She says you haven't forgiven yourself yet. She wants you to know that she is alive. Do you understand?"

The woman shook her head in bewilderment and looked down at the floor.

"She says you have to be happy for Freddie. This little girl likes him, and wants you to be a good grandma to him. She says, 'He wants a happy grandma.' "

All of a sudden I received a very strong impression, and I wasn't sure if it was from the little girl or my Indian guide.

"Freddie will be fine, and so will his brother. Don't worry. The little girl is also fine. You must take care of yourself and forgive yourself, and things will be much easier in your life. Do you understand, please?"

"Yes," she replied. "This is amazing. Just this morning I went to church and asked for a sign that things would be all right. I don't know how to thank you."

"This little girl came a long way to help you to forgive and love yourself. Do that, and you will have thanked me."

I could see a change had already occurred in the woman. There was definitely a sense of lightness that uplifted her previously cold and somber exterior. After such a display of forgiveness and love, the rest of the evening progressed wonderfully. Everyone left the building feeling immensely comforted and encouraged.

Honey, I Am Sorry

It is quite common to have spirits come back to ask forgiveness for something they did or didn't do while on earth. These stories are tragic and painful to hear, but can bring a necessary release. Often, asking forgiveness seems to be the last bit of business that keeps a spirit from moving out of the astral world into a more fulfilling life in Heaven.

This reading also took place at the Body and Soul Conference in Denver, Colorado, in front of about eight hundred people. I always find it a bit more difficult to stay focused with so many people in the room. But I am reassured when spirits line up behind me, and once I completely relax, the communication becomes clear. In a setting with so many people, spirits often bring through messages that are lessons for everyone in the room. That is, even though the message may not be directly personal, most of the people in the room are touched by and can benefit from it.

A spirit came to my side who was about five foot eleven and weighed one hundred and ninety pounds. He wanted to speak to someone in the audience by the name of Kathy. When I asked the spirit for a little more information in order to find Kathy, he then showed me a basement workbench where he used to sit all the time.

I passed on the image to my audience, and a woman raised her hand.

"What is your name, please?" I asked.

"Kathy," she replied.

"Good, okay. He is showing me a workbench with a Tiffany lamp on it. Do you understand this?"

"Yes," she said. "That lamp was always on his workbench. It was his mother's, and he promised he would fix the wire. It was sitting there for ten years, but he never seemed to get around to it."

At that, everyone laughed, for the detail was so human and good evidence of a spirit's presence.

"He is showing me a radio on the bench and an old calendar on the wall. I am being shown a calendar with a snapshot tacked to it. It looks like a black-and-white picture. Unbelievable! Does this make any sense to you?"

The girl shook her head.

I was very frustrated because that was exactly what I saw.

Kathy then bent over and spoke to a woman sitting next

to her. As she whispered something to the woman, I immediately received the impression of "Iris."

"Do you know something about Iris?"

Kathy exclaimed, "Yes. That's my mom here." She nodded to the lady sitting next to her.

I turned my attention to Iris.

"Does any of what I have been saying make sense to you?"

"Yes. The photo is a picture of me. It's been hangin' up there forever. It was taken right after we got married."

"Did this man drink?" I asked.

Iris continued, somewhat embarrassed, "He liked to drink now and then."

I saw an image of a bottle in a drawer. "Did he ever keep gin in the second drawer of his workbench?"

Iris shook her head and smiled. "Yes, we found out after he died. There must have been twenty to thirty bottles there."

The communication began to take on a more serious tone, and the reason why the spirit came to speak became apparent.

"Do you know the name of Mitch?" I asked.

They both nodded their heads.

Iris answered, "That's my husband's name. That's the one you have been talking to."

I started to describe the feelings he was giving me.

"Kathy, this man wants to speak to you. I am sorry, but I need to give out what I get. He is very sorry about how he treated you. He is expressing how he was not the best father. He is telling me about disapproving of your boyfriends. He never wanted you out of his sight. Is that right?"

"Yes, that's true. Never." Kathy began to get emotional.

"Mitch says he was abusive. He says that he would escape by going down to the basement and getting drunk. Do you understand?"

They both nodded their heads in the affirmative.

"Kathy, he is telling me that he didn't attend your wedding. Is that true?"

"Yes. He wouldn't go because of the man I was marrying. He didn't like him."

"He is very sorry for that. He is saying that he didn't speak to you for a long time."

"Yes. We didn't speak for ten years. I never saw him after I got married. I never saw him before he died," she lamented.

"Your father is begging for your forgiveness. He is so ashamed of what he did to you. But not only for that—he is asking you to forgive him for the pain he caused you as a child. Do you understand this?"

Kathy began to cry. She acknowledged the information by nodding her head.

I then turned my attention to Kathy's mother.

"Iris, you are such a saint. This man is telling me that he was very nasty to you. He used to yell at you all the time, and I feel that his abuse destroyed your self-confidence."

Iris spoke softly. "Yes, it did."

"I feel this man did not love himself. I think that deep down he had no sense of appreciation for himself. He feels so badly about himself and his actions. Iris, he is telling me that he used to hit you."

I cringed at the impression I was getting.

Iris bent her head and sighed, "Yes."

Then I received an image of Mitch sitting in the basement. Above his desk was a rack of hunting rifles. He was taking them down one by one and cleaning them. I related this to the two women, and they completely agreed.

❖

"He used to go down there all the time and shine those guns," said Iris.

The next vision was quite devastating.

"I don't mean to upset you, but I feel this man spent a lot of time in the basement looking at those guns and contemplating suicide. I see him putting one into his mouth. Is that correct?"

I had ask them, even though I knew the answer.

They both answered in unison, "Yes."

"He killed himself down in the basement," murmured Iris.

I was very bothered by this image, and it took me several minutes to regain my composure.

"You are both incredible women for having gone through this experience and coming out of it all in one piece."

As I was speaking to them, I was struck again with an intense image of Mitch. When there is such a strong need, very vivid images often come through.

"This man is kneeling down in front of you, Iris. He is holding out his hand to you and is crying. He is telling me that he wants your forgiveness. He was so terrible to you. He says that when you first met, you were like a fresh-cut flower. You were happy and creative, and he destroyed you. He is saying that he poisoned you by never letting you do what you wanted. He was always trying to control you. He is so very sorry."

Iris just shook her head in acknowledgment and said, "I forgive you, Mitch. You tell him that I forgive him. He no longer has to be in pain. I only want him to be happy."

Everyone in the audience was totally amazed and honored at the same time to hear the words of forgiveness from a woman who had been so beaten down all her life. She truly offered Mitch unconditional love.

"Your husband has heard you, and he is crying. He loves you and thanks you. You have put a smile on his face. He is telling me that he misses your turns. Does that make any sense?"

"Yes. I was a dancer when we got married. He used to sit for hours and watch me practice my turns. As a matter of fact, the picture he had pinned to that calendar was one of me doing a turn."

I thanked and blessed Kathy and Iris for sharing such an intimate moment with all of us. I thanked Mitch for having the courage to seek out his family's forgiveness.

Forgive Me, for I Know Not What I Have Done

Every reading that I do is special in its own way. There are some readings that are extremely emotional, while others are incredibly rich with evidential detail. Then there are those readings that combine both fact and emotion, and the effect is nothing less than astounding. Sometimes such an experience can alter a person's life forever. The following is an example of one such session. A man came to see me after his lover had passed away from AIDS. Expecting to hear words only from his companion, he was utterly flabbergasted when individuals from his distant past pierced the veil because of desperate needs to reach him.

Peter, a likable middle-aged gentleman, had come to me after seeing a demonstration of my work at a benefit for AIDS Project Los Angeles. Shortly after I opened his session

❖

with my usual prayer, I saw a blond-haired man standing to my right. He was quite determined to be known.

"There is a man here. He is rather pushy. He really wants to talk and to make sure that he gets through to you. He has blond hair and is very handsome. He has a bright smile, and all I can say is that he seems pushy and aggressive."

Peter seemed to understand the spirit's mannerisms. "You are describing him. That is what he was like."

"This is a very unusual name, but I will say it anyway. Do you know the name of Norris? It sounds like Norris or Morris?"

"Yes, Norris. That is his name," exclaimed Peter.

"Really, hmm," I replied. "Well, he is telling me no. It is Norrie. 'I prefer to be called Norrie.'"

"OK, fine!" I cried out.

I looked over at Peter. I hoped that he didn't think I was being rude to his friend. Peter's mouth dropped wide open. He was amazed at what I was saying.

"That's right. That was his nickname. We always called him Norrie," said Peter.

"He wants to say hello to Nancy. Please send her his love and also a thank-you."

Peter spoke very slowly, trying to digest every word that I had said. "Yes, I will. She is a close friend. She was there when he died."

"He loves her! Lots of fun, he says."

I continued. "He is saying that he loves the gold lamps by the side of the bed, and that he was fooling around with one of them very recently. Yesterday, or the day before. Did you notice a change with one of the lamps, please?" I asked.

"Yes," Peter responded. "As a matter of fact the bulb did

go out on the lamp on the right side of the bed just yesterday. I thought it had to be Norrie because the lamp was on his side of the bed, and I put in that bulb just a week ago."

"That's spirit!" I exclaimed.

I explained to Peter that the love a person has for another can transcend death, and is often revealed through these sorts of electrical occurrences in the house. As the séance continued, Norrie spoke about his death and described how stubborn he was during his illness. He apologized to Peter for taking advantage of his kindness. He also spoke at length about a bank, and the people who worked there. Later Peter confirmed that Norrie had indeed worked at a bank. Halfway through the session, Norrie said that someone else had to speak with Peter. He assured Peter that they would speak again soon, and that he would always be with him in his dreams.

"I have a lady here. She has an English accent and is using the name of Julie."

"Yes, I understand," answered Peter.

"I feel like it's a mother vibration. Is that correct? Has your mother passed?"

"Yes. And that is her name." Peter then began to speak directly to her.

"Hello, Mother. Welcome. Thanks for coming."

I tuned in to this woman's vibration and instantly felt awful. She had come with a very heavy heart and needed some reassurance and love.

"This lady is very upset, Peter. She wants me to tell you how sorry she is. She says that her life was not her own, and she didn't think she could raise you."

Tears began to well up in Peter's eyes.

"She says she is sorry that she was not there for you. She really needs your forgiveness."

❧

"I forgive her. I understand."

"She is confessing that she doesn't feel she was much of a mother to you and wished so much she could have taught you things, especially when you were younger. She is telling me that she knows the pain this has caused you in your life, but in some small way she thinks it might have helped you to become stronger."

"I believe that," Peter responded. "Thinking back on it, it was extremely rough, but it gave me an inner strength and taught me to be self-confident."

"Your mother is very proud of you. She says that you will know her better when it is your turn to come over there. She is telling me, 'My son has a sympathetic heart.' "

Peter smiled.

Then out of the blue came the feeling of another spirit standing in front of me. I tuned in to this new vibration and saw a nun dressed in a black habit with an oversized rosary tied around her midsection.

"I am here to speak with this man, Peter. May I do so, please?" she asked.

I answered. "Yes. Who are you, please?"

"I am Sister Edith. He was a young student of mine. I took care of him when he was a little boy."

I asked Peter if he understood all of this.

"Yes, I do. She raised me," Peter replied.

"She wants me to tell you that she is very, very sorry. She is begging for your forgiveness. She says that she was very mean and cruel to you. She is telling me that she would keep you locked in darkened closets or rooms."

"Yes. It was dreadful," Peter affirmed.

It was a scene that gave me uneasy feelings even as I delivered it to Peter, but I had to continue.

"This nun is telling me that she understands now so

much more than she did on earth. She is saying that she had no patience and was frustrated. She did not want to be in that situation and felt trapped. She turned her anger toward the children."

"You bet she did. She was a horrible lady. You're asking a lot from me to forgive such an individual for what she has done. She must have been in a place she should not have been."

"She is saying that she was pressured by her family," I interjected.

Peter was silent for a minute. "Of course, I forgive her, but it is hard for me to ever forget it."

I proceeded with the session for a little while longer as Sister Edith spoke to Peter and told him that she was learning how to love in the spirit world.

"She is saying thank you for showing your love through your forgiveness."

After the reading, Peter told me that his mother had been a lost soul who had placed him in an orphanage when he was five years old. He lived there with Sister Edith and several other nuns until he left at the age of fifteen.

Peter certainly had a lot of forgiving to do in his life. It was amazing to witness such a letting go of pain as in this beautiful session with Peter, his mother, and Sister Edith.

I often ask people at my demonstrations, "Was there ever a time that you wanted the benefit of the doubt or be forgiven for something you had done?" When I discuss forgiveness, I ask people to try to possibly see things from the other person's perspective. Perhaps we haven't taken a person's situation into consideration. Maybe we don't understand their motives or outlook. Or maybe we have placed our own expectations on the other person. In any case, I always suggest giving another the benefit of the doubt, for it is those who forgive who will be forgiven.

I believe that forgiveness must be an act of grace, unconditional and done with no expectation of the outcome. When we truly forgive another person, we are using the highest aspects of the soul to reopen the inflicted wound and let it be soothed with the wholeness of love. Forgiveness frees the heart and takes us from the position of victim to someone in charge. It helps us to realize our true self.

12

❁

Love

Love is the law of God. You live that you may learn to love. You love that you may learn to live. No other lesson is required of man.

—Mikhail Naimy

What is this thing called love? Is it a natural instinct that we are born with? Is it a behavior that we have to learn and become conditioned to accept? Is it a feeling captured in a lover's gaze? Or is it, perhaps, a mysterious, out-of-reach star—something that we will have to strive lifetimes to attain?

I personally believe that love is *all*. I believe that it is that God Force energy of which we are a part. This force is represented spiritually by the Light, and we are of the Light. The brighter our light, the stronger is our awareness of this part of our nature. We are born with this sense of our light, and are encouraged either to increase it or to hide it from ourselves and from the rest of the world. Some of us lose sight of our light and spend our life searching for poor substitutes for love. Drugs, sex, and violence are some of love's replacements.

When we begin to recognize the light of love within ourselves, it is easier to see it in another. When two people are "in love," they see that light in each other. The world outside does not exist for them because they are in their private world of love, and they feel the splendor and joy that love bestows.

When you begin to live from the inner light of your soul, the deepest center of love, you truly begin to live as a spiritual being. Like someone in love, you experience a relationship with your "heart self." Each time you have a kind thought, say a kind word, or are of service to someone, you are living the divine principle of love, and your love center expands. You start to see the world through loving eyes, and feel the beauty and joy in all things. In essence, you experience heaven on earth.

As I researched my readings to find those that dealt with love, I discovered that I had given myself quite a task. How could I limit love to one particular kind? For love has no limitations, and no one love is more important than any other. Should I depict the love of a mother for her child, or a husband for his wife, or even the love of a devoted pet for its owner? To say the least, it was a difficult decision.

The three readings that I chose revealed acts of love, performed by average people. Each one shows love at its highest level—the willingness to sacrifice or give one's life for another—and had the power to heal and change the recipient, if only he or she would accept the love. I hope that in reading them, your own light will be enriched. As each of us fosters love in our own lives, we are able to pass it on to every life we touch.

❖

An Angel Saved My Life

No one could possibly create a movie or a novel more dramatic or poignant than an average human life. Its twists and turns and the depth of the accompanying emotions would be almost impossible to duplicate. The following story demonstrates this perfectly. It displays the purity of love and a respect for life. In this case, death bound together two people who were practically strangers in life.

It emerged in a séance I conducted in Los Angeles for a nice group of eight individuals. Usually when I do several readings at a time, one in particular will stand out. I feel this one special reading is the reason for my visit in the first place. Often, a spirit will have such a strong need to get a message to a living being that it will go to great lengths to create a situation in which it can be made known.

After reading for four of the eight people present, I was ready for a break. However, I felt compelled to complete one more reading. I looked over at a young man who was sitting at the end of the couch. His name was Andrew. He was about twenty-two with light brown hair, and he was wearing a bright plaid shirt. He seemed very quiet, and I felt that he hadn't come to the séance of his own volition. Later I found out that my hunch was correct. Andrew was present at the insistence of a friend.

When I approached Andrew, he made it clear to me that he wanted to speak to the grandmother who raised him. I concentrated intensely, but was unable to receive any vibrations from his grandmother. Instead, someone very unexpected came through.

"Do you know anything about Chicago?" I asked.

"Yeah, I was born there and lived there when I was very young."

❖

"Hmm . . . Did you go to school there?"

"Yeah, for a little while. Why?" Andrew asked.

"I am getting an impression of a Chicago school, and I am seeing a young boy."

I continued. "Who is Ziggy? That is a very odd name, but that is what I am hearing. Do you understand?"

"Ziggy? I don't know any Ziggy," Andrew responded.

"No, not now. In Chicago, a long time ago," I said.

"No . . . I don't think so."

Andrew hesitated a moment. I could practically hear his brain cells rattling around in his head as he attempted to recall a person named Ziggy. After a few minutes, he still had no clue, so I began once again.

"Wait a minute!" cried Andrew, stopping me in midsentence. "I did know someone . . . Yeah, it was good old Ziggs. We called him Ziggy because of the David Bowie album. We hung out together when we were kids. There were two other guys. One was Mike Barras and another guy . . . I can't remember his name."

"Wyland?" I interrupted with a freshly received thought.

Andrew turned pale as the response "Yes" fell from his lips. His eyes widened. "How did you know that?"

"There is a man standing in front of you who says he knew you at that time of your life. He says he knew you and Ziggy and Wyland."

Andrew was noticeably shaken by my remark. He shook his head in disbelief. "Who is it? Who is this guy? Do I know him?" he asked.

I sent out a mental message to this spirit, asking him to provide me with more identifying details. After a few minutes, I received some thoughts and conveyed them to Andrew.

"This man who stands here gives me the impression that he is a guardian angel of yours. He is concerned about your welfare. He is showing me his hands. I see calluses. He worked with his hands because he is showing me tools now. He is saying that you would know him by the name of Shorty."

Andrew once again racked his brain in an effort to recall this name.

I continued with the impressions I was getting.

"This man Shorty passed over with a heart problem. But he is also showing me smoke. Like a fire."

Andrew let out a shriek. Apparently, I said the secret word!

"Oh, my God!" Andrew's eyes began to well up with tears. "I don't believe it. How the . . . Shorty? Shorty from school?" he cried out.

"Yes, the one from Chicago."

"Arghhhh" shouted Andrew. He held his face in his hands and groaned.

Everyone around Andrew started to pat him on the back and tried to comfort him. He remained in a discombobulated state for a good five minutes. When he composed himself, he lifted his head and began to speak.

"Shorty was the janitor at my grade school. One day there was an explosion in the boiler room, and Ziggy, Wyland, and I got trapped in the basement. Everything was on fire. We were screaming our heads off because we thought we were gonna die. And then we looked up and saw Shorty coming through the smoke. He got us out of there! If it wasn't for Shorty, I wouldn't be here right now. That man saved my life!"

A unanimous "Wow!" rose from the entire room.

"He risked his life for me! I owe him everything.

❖

Thanks, Shorty. I love you, man," Andrew exclaimed as he looked upward.

Then he turned to me. "But why is he around me?"

I had to go into a little explanation about the spirit world.

"When on earth Shorty lived a similar life to the one you are living now. He is here to watch over you and to help you from making the same mistakes he made. He has a genuine concern for your welfare. He is telling me that one of the very positive things he did in his lifetime was to save you and your friends. He wants to make sure that his act of kindness continues in some way. Therefore, he stays around to protect you. He is telling me that he was with you in Springfield. Do you understand Springfield?" I asked.

Andrew bolted upright. "Yeah . . . I got it. I understand now, believe me!"

I listened as Shorty told me some incredible things about Andrew's life. But the information that he relayed would have embarrassed the young man in front of the group.

"I would like to speak with you at the end of the meeting to give you the last bit of information that Shorty is transmitting. It is very personal."

Andrew and I sat together in an adjacent room of the house later that evening, and I finished giving him Shorty's message.

"This man Shorty is extremely concerned about you. He was talking about drugs. He was telling me that you were in the penitentiary in Springfield, and it was a situation that could have been avoided."

"Yeah, I was selling drugs and got busted," admitted Andrew.

"Your friend Shorty came here tonight to help you. He

said you must seek help for the drug addiction and that only you can help yourself."

"Shit! How did he know that? No one here knows that!"

"He said you must stop, or it will be your demise. He wanted you to hear that loud and clear!" I said firmly

Then I looked at Andrew straight in the eye. "Do you understand?"

Andrew began to cry like a baby. I put my arm around him, and together we discussed his predicament.

I don't know whether it was the evidential information or the loving concern from his guardian angel, Shorty, but that night changed Andrew's life forever. He decided right there and then to take responsibility for his life, and told me that he would seek out the necessary counseling and rehabilitation for his drug addiction. Together we thanked Shorty for coming back and snatching Andrew one more time from death's door.

That reading was five years ago. Currently, Andrew lectures to groups in Narcotics Anonymous. He has been instrumental in saving many others' lives, and has in turn become a living angel here on earth.

You Gave Your Life So That I Might Live

A few years ago I agreed to appear on a television show entitled *Paranormal Borderline*. The producers researched hundreds of letters requesting readings until they finally chose one that they felt merited exploration. That's how Tom and Michelle Okins turned up in my living room, amid a herd of technicians setting up equipment.

Tom told me that he had lost his mother when he was five years old. Since then he had been isolated from his family and locked in a long struggle against drugs and alcohol. Several attempts he had made at suicide had failed. At the age of thirty, Tom felt that there was a vital piece of his life missing, and I was his last possible hope at getting it back.

Finally the lighting, stage, and sound were set, and the cameras were ready to roll. I directed the couple to concentrate on me as I in turn relaxed and opened my energy to the spirit world. Soon the two worlds blended, and a spirit's thoughts began to penetrate my mind.

"There is a lady here who is an outgoing person. She doesn't let anyone stand in her way. She is very independent, and in some ways, Tom, you resemble her. Your personality, that is."

I could see that Tom was grasping at every word that I said. He hoped that I could reveal something, anything, that could let him know I was speaking to his mother.

"Yeah, I guess. That is what I have heard about her. I don't remember, of course."

"Do you know if your mother had ties to Oklahoma?" I asked.

"Yeah, ah, that's where she is from. That's where we all lived." Tom's eyes widened in anticipation.

"This lady standing here is talking about your watch, Michelle. She is telling me that it broke. She is saying something about three o'clock."

"Oh, God! Yes. That's right! Just today in the hotel. My watch stopped around three. Look!"

Michelle showed me the broken watch on her wrist. It read 3:15.

The couple stared at each other and squeezed each other's hands.

I took my time with the message about to be revealed. I knew that Tom and Michelle were about to witness a dream come true.

"Tom, I believe the lady standing next to you is your mother. She is extremely excited to talk to you."

Tom bowed his head in gratitude.

"She is so happy to be here. She can hardly contain herself. Michelle, she wants to thank you for taking care of her boy. She is saying that you are the one that saved him. She is indebted to you."

I then turned to Tom and asked, "Who works at a bank?"

"I do," stated Michelle.

"This lady tells me that you won't be there much longer."

"That's so funny," replied Michelle. "I was thinking about getting a different job. I want to be a teacher."

"Well, you will, according to this lady," I exclaimed.

"This lady is showing me a guitar, and she is singing. She is saying that she loves to sing. Do you understand this, Tom?"

"Yes, sir, I do." Suddenly, he began to cry. I handed him a box of tissues, and he wiped his eyes.

After a few minutes he said, "My mom used to play the guitar, as a matter of fact."

Then he searched his pants pocket and pulled out a picture. He showed me a photo of his mother sitting in front of a fireplace strumming a guitar. We all stared at the picture.

By then the whole room was silent. When I looked around the room, I could see faces streaming with tears. Clearly, the technicians had never seen or heard anything like this before.

❖

But just when I thought that we had reached the height of our emotional roller coaster, the spirit revealed a new piece of information.

"Your mother is showing me a country road. There are cornfields on either side of the road. She is driving an old car, and is wearing a big straw hat. She is singing along with the radio."

At this point Tom was crying openly.

"This is very strange, but I keep being shown mailboxes. You know, the kind that are on posts along the side of the road."

Tom began to hiccup, and in between breaths I heard him say, "Yes, that's right, sir. She was going to get the afternoon mail."

All of a sudden I was overcome by an intense image, with the rumble of sound effects.

"Your mom is in the car singing a song as she drives down the road. She looks over to a small boy in the front seat next to her. I hear a plane overhead. It is a sort of crop duster. The sound gets louder. Your mother stops the car. All at once the plane loses control and falls right on top of the car. She pushes the small boy down to the floor just in time because the plane shears off the roof of the car. Your mom is killed instantly. But the boy next to her lives."

Then the vision faded away.

After a few moments Tom looked at me and slowly said, "That boy was me!"

I looked back at Tom and slowly realized what he had said. As I returned to the consciousness of the room, I felt very drained, as though I had been transported back in time and space. I was oblivious to the director screaming, "Cut!"

I continued receiving messages for the sweet young couple.

"Your mother is saying that she loves you very much, and if she had to, she would do it all over again. She wants you to know that her love never stopped. She is saying that you have to realize that she is always with you and always will be."

She went on.

"She is saying that you should not let people take advantage of you. You come from strong stock."

Then she told the couple to expect a little girl of their own. Later, Tom and Michelle told me that they were planning to have a family, and that they would name their daughter after Tom's mother.

A Friend Until the End

This next reading occurred during a metaphysical conference in the Midwest. Such conferences are wonderful opportunities for people with varied interests and belief systems to come together and experience things that are not usually part of their lives. I take a special measure of joy in sharing my gift with people who have never witnessed it.

This particular fall morning was especially joyful: I was able to bring through a spirit who wanted to rekindle a love that had begun on the earth thirty years earlier.

As I looked out at the crowd, I was suddenly led to a red-haired lady sitting on a chair at the very back of the auditorium. Standing right above her was a spirit lady with beautiful sea blue eyes. The spirit was trying very hard to

❖

get my attention. So I told the woman, "I would like to come to you. I have been drawn to you because of a lady standing next to you."

The woman rose to her feet and looked around in bewilderment.

"She has beautiful blue eyes and brown hair," I conveyed.

"Could it be my grandmother? That was how she looked when she was younger," said the woman.

"No," I replied. "That is not the thought that I am being given. This lady knew you when *you* were younger."

Now the woman had a blank expression on her face.

"The lady here is telling me that you and she are closer than you think, and that she loves you very much. She wants me to tell you that she has been growing up with you, and she will always be your friend."

Again, the woman drew a blank.

"Who is Emma?" I asked.

"That's me," she replied.

"This woman is showing me dolls and a dollhouse. Do you understand this?"

Without hesitation Emma responded, "No, sorry. Are you sure I'm the one you want?"

I concentrated on the thoughts of the spirit and requested that it send through more in the way of identification.

"This lady tells me that you used to love to comb her hair. She is saying that you wished that you had hair like hers."

Emma was beginning to recognize something I had said. It seemed that she had to search her mind for some far-off, distant lifetime, but slowly the memories were returning.

"I think I know who it is," she murmured.

"This woman is talking about the operation," I continued.

Emma let out a piercing scream and began to sob.

"Patty?" she asked.

"She is not giving me her name at the moment, but she is telling me that you may remember sharing a ride with her on an ice cream truck."

"Yes, it's Patty. Her father drove a Good Humor truck, and he used to give us a ride on it after dinner. We used to take turns ringing the bell. Oh, my God, Patty. I love you. Oh, Patty, thank you. How can I ever thank you?"

Patty's thoughts continued to pour through me.

"She loves you as well and always will. She is telling me that you are a part of her, and you always will be."

I thought that Patty was expressing that she would always be at her friend's side. I didn't realize there was something more to what she was telling me.

"Yes, that is right. If it weren't for Patty, I might not be here right now."

"Why is that?" I asked.

Through her tears, Emma began to tell her story.

"When we were children, I had a rare kidney disease and needed a kidney to survive. Because of our compatibility and ages, Patty was the perfect donor. Patty decided to give me her kidney because she had just learned that she had leukemia. We made sort of a joke about it. She would tell me that she didn't need her kidney where she was going, and that I better take good care of it or she would come back and take it away from me."

No one in the room was prepared for this bit of information. Suddenly, the dead silence was broken by an onslaught of applause. People applauded for the great love of a little friend who had given part of herself so that her best friend could live.

After that, I had to stop reading for the day. I was too

emotionally charged—and so was the audience—by Patty's profound act of love.

So, you see, love is so far-reaching that it transcends death. Love is the strongest force in the universe. When given correctly, it unifies and builds, defends and protects. It is a concentrated energy that has no boundaries. True love is never jealous or possessive, nor does it have conditions. I think that we experience life after life to learn about love and see it manifest in different ways in different circumstances. How else could we appreciate the many facets of our being?

PART THREE

THE
AWAKENING

13

❋

Remembering the Real You

The eye must be something like the sun,
Otherwise no sunlight could be seen;
God's own power must be inside us,
How else could Godly things delight us?
—Johann Wolfgang von Goethe,
Something Like the Sun

We are currently on the brink of the twenty-first century, a time of incredible breakthroughs, such as global communications, gene therapy, and numerous others in the fields of science and technology. Never before have human beings been so well linked to each other, yet never have people seemed so alone. Everywhere you look, you see people who are unfulfilled and unhappy. They appear to be robotic and self-involved, just going through the motions of existing. Others are enslaved by anger, ill health, depression, fear, greed, and hate. Why is this? I believe it is because of the value system of our society, which is based on illusions and falsehoods. We have been taught to respect the pursuit of money and that being wealthy is synonymous with being happy and content. We

❖

have been taught that wealth equals power and that power can fulfill us. In honoring these false gods of power and money, society constantly emphasizes our inadequacies.

And what about people in power? We are forever placing humans on pedestals, expecting them to be perfect, and when they are not, we feel betrayed. We give our power to others, and then when they don't do something we like with it, we feel victimized. Once we declare ourselves "victims," we become locked in a vibration of retribution. When we live in fear, anger, and resentment, we attract situations that will create still more fear, anger, and resentment. The more involved we are in the consciousness of the outer world, the further we stray from the path of spirit.

There is a tremendous spiritual deficit in our world. It is a hunger that is not being met. Ideally, religion should be the gateway to our spirituality, but too often this is not so. It takes more than going to church, praying, singing, preaching, and giving money to be spiritual. It takes a comprehension of the spiritual truths, and putting them into action in our daily lives. Unfortunately, sometimes the truths taught by religion are distorted by personal interpretation, and fear of God comes to substitute for serving God. It is left to each of us as individuals to sort out the truth from the dogma, to cull the wheat from the chaff.

Spiritually minded individuals have always thought for themselves, but today too many people have forgotten who they are. They want happiness, love, and joy, and they keep searching outside themselves to find these qualities. They do not realize that although we are living in a physical world and have physical sensations, we have something more real, more powerful that is deep inside us.

We are not here to be enslaved by the tenets of a society that dwell on the lower and negative aspects of the earthly personality. We must stop living a life based on guilt, worry, and fear. The time has come for us to reacquaint ourselves with the meaning of God and to envision ourselves as spiritual beings of light and love.

You are and always will be a spark of the Divine. Never forget it. Your home is Heaven, and you journey to this earth to do your homework. Life on earth is temporary. The key to walking on this planet is a keener awareness of your spiritual heritage. When you live every day seeing the world with spirit in mind, you are living a life of truth.

The body is just a repository of bones, tissues, and organs. By itself it has no life. It is the soul that gives your body its life and creative expression. When your spiritual self is empowered, you can begin to experience the fullness of life.

If we are to learn from the examples of the spirit world, we must begin to take responsibility for every aspect of our lives. We are the only ones who can change the way we think and act. When we make decisions that are positive and for our growth, even when such decisions seem difficult, we become active participants in our lives. Then life will not just happen to us. To reawaken and reconnect with our soul essence, we must exercise our spiritual muscles, and the most effective way is through meditation.

Meditations

When I am teaching in a large auditorium in front of hundreds of people, I often begin with the following statement: "I'm sorry, but I do not levitate off the stage or spit out any green pea soup. I do not speak in foreign tongues, nor will you hear any grunts and groans emanating from my person. If you want to see these sorts of things, I suggest you see a movie or rent a video." I say it in jest to get a point across. Through many years of working with individuals who have strong spiritual or metaphysical backgrounds, I am still amazed that the majority do not know how to stay in their bodies. They do not realize the importance of being in the present moment while focusing their awareness in spirit. People seem to believe that in order to be spiritual, one must be blissed out or in an altered state. This is not true at all. In fact, when people space out and leave the body (whether consciously or unconsciously), they open themselves up to energy vibrations from any level. Mostly, they are targets for the lowest elements of consciousness, as these are closest to the earth. I have discussed the idea of earthbound entities. These entities like to visit or intrude into our energy fields and bodies.

Focusing your awareness on the spirit means staying in the present, in your body, and taking control of your physical space. I like to call it being the driver of your own vehicle.

What follows are some exercises to help you gain mastery over your thoughts and emotions. They will help you to clear and strengthen your aura and to remember who you are. I have adapted the following two techniques from the work of a very talented healer and metaphysician, my friend Michael Tamura. First, and most important, remember that everything involves awareness or where and what you focus on. When you think of something, you give it life. Begin each meditation in an atmosphere where you will not be bothered by outside distractions, such as phones, answering machines, doorbells, etc. The best way to do any meditation is to sit in a comfortable chair with your back straight and your feet flat on the floor. This helps to align the chakras of your etheric body so that you are receptive to the higher vibrations.

Grounding

Close your eyes. Become aware of your body. Listen to the body. Be aware of every movement of the body. Now place your focus on the breath that brings refreshing and rejuvenating new life into the lungs as it releases old, stagnant energy that you no longer need. Take several deep breaths, and enjoy every new breath you take. After a few minutes of deep breathing, place your focus on the body. Be aware of every part of your body. With your mind's eye, sense each part of the body, starting at the feet, then your legs, hips, buttocks, pelvic area, stomach, chest, back, hands, arms, shoulders, neck, and head. Envision two cords gently tied around each ankle. Bring these cords straight down through the center of the earth. Imagine two big boulders in the earth's center, and tie each cord to a boulder. Now tie another cord around your tailbone and direct that cord toward the center of the earth. Find another boulder of your liking, and tie this cord around it.

Next, visualize Mother Earth's energy. You may see this energy as green or brown. See the energy rising up the cords from the boulders in the center of the earth to around your ankles. This energy continues to flow up the legs and torso and moves into the center of your heart. Now you are full of earth energy. You will feel grounded, centered, and stabilized. It is important to have a balance of energy. The next step is to bring in cosmic energy.

Imagine a golden-white beam of light about three inches above your head. This represents the cosmic or Christ light. Bring this cosmic light through the top of your head, and see it meld into the head, neck, shoulders, and chest. Let it travel down into the heart center. There the cosmic light intermingles with the earth energy and forms a new, stronger stabilizing force. To finish, visualize this newly mingled energy rising up the spine and out the top of your head, and then cascading down the sides of your body like an overflowing fountain of energy.

Visualize the commingling of the energy over and over again. This is the way to run new and recharged energy throughout your body's energy systems. Once this meditation is completed, you can begin to do your spiritual work in a more controlled and mindful atmosphere.

Protection

Because we live in a world where we constantly receive the thoughts and feelings of others, we need to guard ourselves against negative influences that may intrude into our daily lives. This is especially helpful for those of us who are sensitive sponges and pick up another person's energy quite easily. Although it is impossible to entirely dissipate others' energies and thought forms, this technique will strongly assist in clearing them away from your space and your consciousness.

Begin as you did the previous exercise. Sit once again in a chair, your back straight. Perform the breathing techniques as directed. Go through the entire grounding exercise first because this helps to reinforce your auric field.

After you have energized your field, I want you to see or sense a small vacuum cleaner in the palm of your hand. It can be one of your own design. Now place your focus on the space around the top of your head. As you do, notice what appears in your mind's eye. Do you see the faces of others? Do you feel emotions that you can't recognize or don't belong to you? Take your vacuum and clean away those images and feelings. You can even view them going up the hose into the machine if that is easier. Once your vacuum bag is full, blow it up. Send the energy back to its originator with love. Create a new vacuum to clean every spot in your energy field. Vacuum out the front, back, sides, top, and bottom of your space. Create as many vacuums as you need. It may take one cleaning, or it may take many more. Continue until you begin to feel much lighter and happier.

Now that you have removed others' energy from you, it's time to get yours back. Imagine every place you have been in the last twenty-four hours. See where you left your energy. Perhaps you were talking to someone on the phone. Perhaps you were at work. Maybe you left it at school or in a store. Recall any place where you may have left a residue of your energy. See the situation and the people involved, and take your energy back. Pull it back into your space. See your energy coming back into your body through the top of your head and flowing down your spine. It comes in like star dust. Feel yourself filling up with your own energy. It feels so good to get back all the energy that you gave away so freely. Once you have a strong sense that your energy is back home, it is time to visualize a wall of protection around you.

You can do this in several ways. You can imagine a cloak of your own design and color totally wrapped around you. You can visualize yourself standing in either a glass or stone box with a glass ceiling. It is harder for thoughts and energies to penetrate these walls. Many people place themselves in white light, which is a great protector as well. But remember, as you use these techniques, what is out stays out, and what is in stays in. Therefore, make very sure that you have completely cleaned away all foreign energies prior to setting up a wall of light and protection around you. Many people also use symbols such as a cross or six-pointed star. Remember that as you focus, you give life to your thoughts. Protect yourself with your intention. Symbols are merely devices to reinforce your intention.

Bringing Out Your Light

The realization of the light of which you are made is a vital and healthful necessity for living in the physical world. I very often use this simple technique with people who have lost touch with their inner light and feel as though life has nothing left to offer. After using this technique for a period of time, my clients have told me that their lives and attitudes were altered to a more positive outlook. It is a blessing to share it with each one of you.

Begin once again with the previous two exercises. Once you have grounded and protected yourself, your mind should be in a very receptive and aware state.

Visualize yourself sitting in a garden of your own making. Create your environment, as you want it. Perhaps you have chosen various colored flowers and trees. Add to your garden a lake, some benches, and any items that create the environment you wish to experience. Everyone is different. Some like rose bushes, while others might want lilacs. It doesn't matter. I just want you to look around and be in the garden of your own choosing.

In your garden stands a tree off in the distance. A mirror hangs from this tree. Go up to the tree and look in the mirror. Now look more deeply into the mirror. See right through its surface. Go inside the reflection. As you become one with the reflection of yourself, see yourself as you are now at the present time. See your face and body. Observe as much detail as you can. As you stare at your reflection, bring into focus all the expectations placed on you from others. See areas of your life where you need to be forgiven. See people in your life that you need to forgive. Bring into the reflection all those situations about which you feel guilty.

Now bring in love. See those people or situations and place your love there. See the pink light of love rising out of the center of your heart and touching everyone and everything. Let love touch every part of you as well. Love is you. You are made of love.

Now step away from the mirror, and see yourself standing in your garden. The flowers are brighter and larger; the birds are singing with joy all around you. The sky is filled with colors of the heart, and you are aware of yourself as a loving, spiritual entity who can create the life you want. Look at the sun, and see it as a reflection of you. You are the Light. Now that you have realized this, you can never hide it again, for it needs to shine and touch everyone it encounters.

14

❀

Guiding Our Children

> And I made a rural pen,
> And I stained the water clear,
> And I wrote my happy songs
> Every child may joy to hear.
> —William Blake, Introduction
> to *Songs of Innocence*

O ne of the most important ways to transform our world is by fostering growth and expansion in our children. As spirits we are born into families with whom we have had many karmic ties. Each member has chosen another as part of his and her life plan. One by one we pick our respective roles of father, mother, sister, brother, daughter, son, aunt, uncle, and so on. With all players in place, the play commences.

Bringing up children in today's toxic world is extremely difficult. Children are exposed to violence, drugs, and sex as never before. Values seem to have run amuck. But it is also true that at the very same time, when things seem to be reeling out of control, we are in a period of incredible potential for enlightenment and expansion. Children can develop their mental capacities much faster than ever. The results are brighter and more aware beings to carry on in the future. When people decide to have children, they have an obligation not only to sustain life on a physical level, but also to encourage the spiritual and emotional bodies as well. On these levels a baby is like a psychic sponge soaking up all the impressions that are present in the environment.

Therefore, parents need to realize that they are responsible for the feelings and thoughts they give out because this energy passes directly into a child's psyche. Such conditioning is carried like baggage into adulthood. How many of us are still hearing messages from our parents, even though they are miles away or gone? Because of our interrelation with one another, we need to start teaching our children dignity, values, and priorities by our example.

I have worked with children in many capacities, from camp counselor to teacher and spiritualist, and time after time I have found one common thread throughout my work with them—they copy their parents. Children will usually repeat the words and actions of Mommy and Daddy. So many times in my readings, problems of insecurity, worthlessness, and distrust stem from upbringing. In these situations, parents have not fulfilled their responsibilities.

The following are some guidelines that I would like to share with you about bringing up a child in a spiritually enriching atmosphere. Although I suggest these to parents, I believe all of us could use them, whether we are grandparents, aunts, uncles, teachers, religious leaders, babysitters, or just the neighbors next door.

❖

1. Encourage and Nurture Self-esteem

I cannot begin to emphasize enough the importance of nurturing self-esteem. In nine out of ten readings that I have done that involved a suicide or drug or alcohol addiction, the origins are a lack of self-identity and love of self. What reference point does a child have, if not the actions and words of the adults around him? How are our children supposed to know who they are? What do we say to them, think about them, and do to them? Are they loving messages or put-downs? Do we validate their instincts or shut them up? If children don't have understanding and empathy at home, they will seek it from someone or something outside the family; of that we can be certain. They will turn to television, movies, and friends for some inkling of individuality and assurance. When they begin to identify with outer, illusionary influences for validation, they will be inevitably disappointed. Not only disappointed, but also they will grow up with materialistic attitudes and values. Peer pressure will force them to act out certain behaviors in order to be accepted and validated.

I suggest that parents and relatives give as much positive enforcement as possible to children. We need to demonstrate love. As babies they were held and touched and smiled at. As they grow older, let's not forget to hug them and tell them we love them, especially when they go to school and get busy with activities and friends. Praise, understanding, laughter, and love make a child grow up to be a resourceful and whole adult. Let us all be a source of true enlightenment and guidance for the younger generation.

2. Get to Know Your Child

Do as much as you can to be involved in a child's life. If she likes a particular type of music, take an interest in it even if you don't "understand" it. Take time off during the week to do something special together. Be aware of your child's moods and behavior. A parent should be attentive enough to be able to tell if a child is having a problem. So many times, after a child gets into trouble, parents admit to a lack of awareness. They were either too busy or too indifferent to notice a change in their child's behavior until it was too late. Pay attention, trust your instincts, and above all, talk to your children. Help them to resolve their dilemmas. This will not only encourage a sense of closeness but also reaffirm trust.

3. Be a Best Friend

Friends are always there to help out or show the way. You can discuss anything and everything with friends. As a parent, hopefully you know your children well enough to be a best friend. Speak on their level of understanding while still being aware of your position as parent. Help them to make healthy choices of their friends without judgment or condemnation. Continue building that trust and the bond that was created during the birth process.

4. Teach Self-respect and Responsibility

This goes hand in hand with self-esteem and self-identity. Children have to be taught responsibility, and the best way to teach is your own personal example. Do you take responsibility for your actions, or do you inevitably blame someone or something else when things go wrong?

Our country has become so litigious that I often wonder if anyone wants to take responsibility for his actions. Children have to be gently guided in the proper and healthy ways to treat themselves and others. Assist them in making decisions by giving them suggestions as to what an outcome could be. Distinguish between the ones that will be beneficial or detrimental. Our children pick up on everything, especially what they see on TV. When teaching your children responsibility, give them small tasks to accomplish at first. When completed, honor them and their successes, and discuss failures in a positive way so they can learn from them.

5. Be Open-minded and Spiritually Aware

I have found the best parents are those who are broad-minded and have a variety of interests, which gives them a greater scope of understanding when providing guidance. It is important for parents to share their insights about their own growth experiences with their children.

The spiritual life of children is so overlooked or negated. Educate children in the realization that they are spiritual beings working through lessons of self-awareness. If they have "visions," or dreams, or visits from their "unseen" friends, please don't say, "It's just a dream," and dismiss it. Visions and dreams need to be nurtured and used. Ask them to describe their dreams, even if you don't understand dreams yourself. You might be surprised how much a dream reveals once you start listening. Children are extremely sensitive and clairvoyant. Above all, never invalidate or discourage this type of behavior.

6. *Remember That Children Are Watching You*

The first and foremost way to teach someone is by example. In other words, you teach by the way *you* live your life. Children are great at mimicking. You must treat yourself with love and respect if you expect your child to follow suit. You are their mirror to the outside world and must demonstrate the qualities and principles by which you would like them to live. If you drink and do drugs, expect your child to do the same. If you swear and curse at others, expect your child to follow in your footsteps. And if you beat up on yourself, feel depressed a lot, or spend all your time working or shopping for material goods, and little time on spiritual matters, it is likely that the apple won't fall far from the tree. It is not only confusing to a child when parents say one thing and act differently, but after a while children lose trust in them.

7. *Teach Your Child Self-reliance*

One of the first things children must learn is that they live in an imperfect world. Although to our human mind, life does not always seem fair, on a spiritual level everything is happening for a purpose. Encourage children to use their free will to change what they don't like so that the world can become a better place to live. But teach them that, like us, they must begin to change from within, from their own God-awareness. Give them the spiritual keys to a happy and fulfilling life.

8. Celebrate Individuality

Instill in your child from the beginning the belief that she is not like anyone else on this planet. Children are born with innate wisdom and God-given talents all their own. This not only distinguishes them from everyone else, but also forces them to view the world in their unique way. You will be able to assist in influencing some parts of their behavior, but won't be able to mold and shape them into exactly what you want. Never compare them to anyone else, for that breaks their spirit.

Overall, treat your child as you would a flower or plant. The seed for "self" is present in the child, but, like any flower or plant, it needs to be fertilized, watered, sheltered, and cared for. Watch the flower flourish the moment you acknowledge its beauty and life. Celebrate the God Force energy we all share. With a bit of patience, fun, and encouragement, watch your child shine.

Encourage their self-worth by reminding them that they are unique, special beings made of God's love. Enrich and celebrate their individuality and their presence on this earth.

15

❀

Keys to the Higher Life

Lives of great men all remind us
We can make our lives sublime,
And, departing, leave behind us
Footprints on the sands of time.
—Henry Wadsworth Longfellow,
Resignation

We possess all the spiritual treasures necessary to live full, productive, and happy lives, and these ideals can also help us reach a higher state of consciousness. When we awaken to them, we will never want for anything, as God is abundance personified. There is a limitless supply of love and riches stored up in Heaven that we can bring to earth.

We are blessed every day by the presence of spirit in everything we encounter. I am referring to the spirit within that is constantly fulfilling every need and desire. How we tap into the spirit is up to each of us as an individual. What we put in motion is returned to us. Remember that we are always moving through an invisible sea of thoughts. God will always give us what we ask for based on our thoughts.

If our thoughts dwell on poverty and illness, we will draw these conditions to us. If we elevate our thoughts to a higher frequency level, we will reap harmony and abundance. This is a fixed universal law that cannot be changed.

Is it natural for everyone to live a completely harmonious and abundant existence? Yes, in truth, this is so. If one does not live this way, one must reevaluate his and her thoughts to find out why not. It is up to us to think in the most positive of ways so that we can help ourselves and others around us, whether they are loved ones or strangers.

The world outside is merely a reflection of the world you have created inside.

You are the creator of your own circumstances. When you understand this, you can never become a victim of any situation. What follows are some keys that can help elevate our thoughts. Over the years I have used them as a treasure map to find myself. I hope that you, too, will learn to use them and make them an integral part of your life, to open the treasure chest within.

Keys

Patience

Patience is a rare commodity in today's world. Everyone seems to want everything right now! Aggressive and impulsive behaviors are appreciated especially in business, sports, and entertainment. But we really miss the spiritual boat, so to speak, when we try to make things happen. Everything comes to us in its own time. I don't mean that we have to become apathetic or dismiss opportunities when they show up. Quite the contrary! When you possess patience, you are really in control of your environment. You decide the appropriate time to act, and when not to act, in order to encompass the full range of possibilities available. Patience teaches self-control by the conservation of energy. With this energy you have the power to make decisions that are for your good. I always suggest to students to "meditate on it" before acting, to allow spirit to come through with guidance and information.

When you act or react impatiently, you actually can have an adverse effect on a situation. Sometimes, the best course is to do nothing and let the situation mature and develop in its natural way. As you learn to be more patient, you will feel less stressed and scared about life, and more mindful about the decisions you make.

Wisdom

Wisdom is knowing that God-consciousness resides within you, and you have all the love, light, and power of the infinite at your disposal. In order to be wise, you must become fully aware of the laws of the universe and live your life in accordance with these universal laws. Wisdom does not come from a book but through the experiences of lifetime after lifetime. Each experience is embedded in your soul consciousness to be perfected through the course of your lives on earth. It is an irony of life that the wiser you become, the more you realize how little you really know.

Courage

To have courage, you must believe in yourself. I'm not talking about an egotistical attitude; I am referring to a belief in the power within you.

A courageous person has an awareness of the greater picture and knowledge of the divine plan. With trust and perseverance, all of us can have the courage to hear the inner voice and to follow it. A person who possesses courage is willing to open his heart to others and be vulnerable to life's unpredictable changes.

With courage we always have an ability to face obstacles because we know that infinite possibilities are ever present. Courage gives us the trust we need to follow our hearts no matter what outside influences seem to block our way.

Balance

Balance is another quality that seems to be missing from many people's lives in today's fast-paced world. It seems so much easier to let the lower parts of our natures dominate and gain importance. To bring balance into our lives we must harmonize the material or earthly self with the spiritual self. Excessiveness in any part of our beingness, whether it is emotional, mental, spiritual, or physical, tends to weaken rather than strengthen us. When we are out of balance in any area of our lives, we tend to operate out of fear rather than love.

Discernment

You need a lot of discernment nowadays to see the truth in all things. Too many get caught up in the thoughts and feelings of the mass consciousness, and are unable to see the forest for the trees. When you rush to criticize and judge without having all the facts of a situation, you learn very little. I suggest that you always question what lies behind any person or situation to make sure there is a spiritual truth at the core.

Faith

We all have heard the expression, keep the faith. But faith is ethereal and difficult to grasp onto. Once again, it is an awareness that we are forever supplied with all that we desire and need. Faith is a belief in the unseen nature of the universe. Faith goes hand in hand with trust. When you have faith in yourself and faith in God, you know that you are safe and loved and never alone. You believe in your spiritual nature and know that all things are possible through creative thought. Learn to have faith and trust in the light of your soul.

Creativity

Creativity is the ability to form ideas, feelings, and expressions that can transform the physical world in one way or another. It is a component of the light of God of which we are all made, and not limited to artists, musicians, or writers. Therefore, we are all creative and can use this divine energy in everything to make life easier. Whenever there is a problem in relationships, family, career, finances, or any part of our daily living, we have the ability to resolve the situation through our innate creative spark. God is a bountiful source of ideas and expressions. There is always some way to lighten our load. Creativity also gives life. It frees up energy blocks in our various bodies and helps to bring balance into our lives. When we use our creativity, we use the

❖

God Force energy at its highest possible manifestation, especially when we harness creativity for the highest good of humankind.

Joy and Laughter

We seem to equate spirituality with severity. But being spiritually disciplined does not mean that we have to live a serious life. I find that people with a sense of humor have more joy and give more joy to others. Seeing the brighter and lighter side in all things helps to keep the child within oneself alive and happy. If we are living a God-filled life, it is only natural that we would express joy, laughter, enthusiasm, and happiness.

After all, how can we give the dense, mundane material world so much importance? Remember that our spirit body is light and buoyant; only our physical world is heavy and fixed. Why get bogged down in temporary earthly conditions? When we discover the humor and delight in God's world, we feel the joys of spirit.

Love

Love is the greatest component of life. It unifies everything. It attracts and draws to us all that is good. Through love we become more aware and responsive to the needs of humanity. We see the oneness, commonality, and the spark of God in each person. We can begin with our family, friends, and coworkers. We can love them even if we think they have done something wrong. We can be there for them. That is how we demonstrate our love.

I always say the word *good* contains the word *God*. Love is the closest thing we have on this earth to heaven. Love demonstrates God. This divine, comforting, and healing power is the building block for everything on this earth. Without love we have nothing. We cease to exist.

The spiritual path will not always be smooth; it will inevitably be filled with detours or dead ends. But on it, remember, you never travel alone. Your enlightened family and guides of the spirit world are always with you to provide assurance and guidance.

You are here to manifest God's love in all that you do. Many times it will feel easier to go along with the desires of the lower self, but be patient. Don't succumb to the waves of mass consciousness. Seek truth even when many attempt to fill your head and your heart with falsehoods. Never compromise your spiritual ideals, because that hinders your progress. Never forget that you are an eternal child of God.

Above all, follow your heart and be true to yourself. Never live the life of another. You have to create your own road. Remember that you have a responsibility to be the best you can possibly be, so keep your mind and heart open to the higher aspects of your being. You are the light. As you journey, may you be filled with spirit.

Use your spiritual awareness to encourage and comfort others. As we lift up, enlighten, and love others, we help those who are shackled by their own illusions, judgments, and misconceptions. We show them the keys to their own beautiful inner light.

Shine your light to the far ends of the earth so that everyone can see it. When you do, your journey here will have been worth it. Then you can return to Heaven with the knowledge that you have done your part in bringing God's energy to earth. You will know that you, one soul, have left the world a better place.

Bibliography

Bendit, L. J. *The Etheric Body of Man: The Bridge of Consciousness.* Wheaton, Ill.: Theosophical Publishing House, 1982.

Besant, Annie. *Man and His Bodies.* Wheaton, Ill.: Theosophical Publishing House, 1912.

Edwards, Harry. *Life in Spirit.* Great Britain: Harry Edwards Spiritual Healing Sanctuary Trust, 1976.

Goldsmith, Joel S. *Living Between Two Worlds.* Austell, Ga.: I-Level Publications, 1974.

Guiley, Rosemary Ellen. *Harper's Encyclopedia of Mystical and Paranormal Experiences.* New York: HarperCollins, 1991.

Hall, Manly Palmer. *Reincarnation: The Cycle of Necessity.* Los Angeles: Philosophical Research Society, 1946.

Hampton, Charles. *The Transition Called Death.* Wheaton, Ill.: Theosophical Publishing House, 1982.

Kardac, Allen. *Book on Mediums.* Boston: Colby and Rich, 1874.

❀

Lewis, James R. *Encyclopedia of Afterlife Beliefs and Phenomena*. Detroit: Gale Research, 1994.

Montgomery, Ruth. *A World Beyond*. Greenwich, Conn.: Fawcett, 1971.

Perkins, James S. *Through Death to Rebirth*. Wheaton, Ill.: Theosophical Publishing House, 1982.

Riland, George. *The New Steinerbooks Dictionary of the Paranormal*. New York: Rudolf Steiner Publications, 1980.

Wambach, Helen. *Life Before Life*. New York: Bantam, 1979.

Weiss, Brian L. *Many Lives, Many Masters*. New York: Simon & Schuster, 1988.

White Eagle. *Spiritual Unfoldment 3: The Way to Inner Mysteries*. Great Britain: White Eagle Publishing Trust, 1987.

Whitton, Joel L., and Fisher, Joe. *Life Between Life*. New York: Warner, 1986.

Zubko, Andy. *Treasury of Spiritual Wisdom*. San Diego: Blue Dove, 1996.

For further information regarding James Van Praagh,
you may contact his website at www.VanPraagh.com

Or write to:

Spiritual Horizons, Inc.
P.O. Box 60517
Pasadena, California 91116